# a pocket guide to orchids

# a pocket guide to orchids

Photography by
Greg Allikas

Text by
Ned Nash

GREENWICH
EDITIONS

This edition published in 2004 by
Greenwich Editions
The Chrysalis Building
Bramley Road, London W10 6SP

An imprint of **Chrysalis** Books Group

Produced by
PRC Publishing Limited
The Chrysalis Building
Bramley Road, London W10 6SP

An imprint of **Chrysalis** Books Group



ISBN 0 86288 602 3

Printed and bound in Malaysia

# CONTENTS

# INTRODUCTION

The last decade of the 20th century has seen unprecedented growth in the popularity and visibility of orchids in all sectors of the American scene. From the most upscale architectural and lifestyle publications, to the bargain racks of the "big box" merchandisers, consumers are never far from the sight of flowering orchid plants. Once exclusively the hobby of the wealthy or eccentric, flowering orchids now grace the homes of the middle class almost as a decorative afterthought. If you flick through the pages of any glossy magazine, you can see lovely orchids—individual plants or exotic arrangements—as a part of the décor favored by the rich and famous. Prior to World War 2, orchid nurseries catered exclusively to those wealthy people who could afford to spend lavishly on the flowers or the plants. Yet now we can walk down the aisle of nearly any garden center in the land and purchase a magnificent orchid in flower for only $19.99, that once might have sold for $50 or $150 or $500—if it had even been for sale.

In the early years of the hobby—nearly 200 years ago now—there were no nurseries growing orchids at all. Collecting started when wealthy British landowners began to expand their knowledge of the new worlds being discovered and settled, and their interest in the richness and diversity of the flora and fauna in these strange lands. Only a few orchid enthusiasts were rich enough to travel to collect them where they grew in their native habitats, so those

Above and Right: *Colm.* Wildcat

who couldn't go themselves, sponsored collectors to return with these exotic treasures, and a hobby began to first take shape.

The Duke of Devonshire was the first to have the "orchid sickness," contracting it just after the turn of the 19th century at an exhibition of exotic plants. When he saw *Oncidium* (now *Psychopsis*) *papilio* in flower, its blooms resembling nothing so much as immense, brightly colored butterflies, he was hooked. His personally financed collecting expeditions to orchid-rich habitats were soon joined by those of his status-conscious peers. Orchid collections were tended by specially apprenticed growers, many of whom later joined forces with the collectors to form the first exotic nurseries. The main drawback was that the orchids had to be directly collected from their native habitats, as their growth from seed was sporadic and chancy.

Shortly after World War I, a researcher at Cornell University, Dr. Lewis Knudson, discovered the link between the symbiotic fungal invasion of orchid seed and its successful germination. Even as his technique spread to both sides of the Atlantic, orchid nurseries and the men who ran them remained autocratic and secretive, catering to the needs of their aristocratic patrons alone—whether for flowers or for plants. Newly developed hybrids were often worth nearly their weight in gold; but the public was not welcome. The only real dissension ever experienced in the leadership cadre of the American Orchid Society was between factions who were split on whether or not growing techniques ought to be publicized. Unfortunately for those outside this exclusive circle, the group supporting information dissemination lost.

Despite the best efforts of the autocrats, orchid growing as a hobby of the middle class became inevitable after World War 2. The rapid growth in production of orchid seedlings initially intended to supply cut flowers to a burgeoning market created by the industrialization of World War 2, coupled with the

resultant rise in expendable income and free time, led to a happy marriage of opportunity and demand.

Orchid plants—surplus to a cut-flower demand suddenly cut short by the end of hostilities—soon became available at prices within the range of the common man.

Local orchid societies sprang to life and orchid shows grew in popularity as well as in demand, as marketing venues for newly emergent hobbyist-oriented nurseries. Wealthy businessmen began to see their formally exclusive hobby as an opportunity for business-related tax write-offs, if not for profit. The young men and women who grew their orchids became entrepreneur heroes of a new generation of orchid-hungry amateurs.

The 1950s, 1960s and 1970s saw a starburst of imaginative hybridizing and attendant merchandising. Cloning of select orchid varieties—many of which were rare and fetched prices in the hundreds or thousands of dollars—became a practical reality, bringing beautiful and rare cultivars within the grasp of just about any hobbyist.

Still, the orchid hobby, though truly within the reach of millions, was limited to perhaps tens or hundreds of thousands of dedicated initiates. The American Orchid Society's membership grew from a

Above: *Psy. papilio.*

few thousand immediately after World War 2, to 17,000 in the mid-Eighties (it now approaches 30,000.) Orchids became increasingly easily available for those willing to look for them by traveling dozens or even hundreds of miles to visit specialized orchid nurseries. Flowering divisions of plants surplus to cut flower needs—usually cattleyas or cymbidiums—became seasonally available in areas where they were grown. But for most gardeners, orchids retained a reputation as being difficult-to-grow plants suitable only for the rich. Meanwhile, orchid growers discussed which would come first, the chicken or the egg? Would merchandising come first, or would a grower take the gamble to ramp up the production necessary to penetrate the mass market? What varieties would perform best for this mass market? How could they ever become a cost-effective crop? What means could be used to safely distribute the flowering plants without unacceptable cost add-ons?

Why have orchids suddenly burst upon the public consciousness? What factors have enabled them to become the Cinderella story of horticulture? Why are conservation groups seizing upon orchids to serve as the pandas of habitat conservation? What is it about orchids that make ordinarily intelligent and functional people into fanatic collectors, unable to resist "just one more?" Why are law-abiding citizens willing to become criminals just to have the most recently discovered orchids in their possession? Why would anyone spend tens of thousands of dollars for just one plant? Finally, why do orchid hobbyists look knowingly at each other and wink, when one of their previously uninitiated friends announces they've just been given their first orchid?

The story of orchids—their biology, their history in cultivation, their economics and industry, the people and sociology around them—is every bit as fascinating as their varied floral shapes, colors, and perfumes. The stories in this book, along with Greg Allikas' extraordinary photography, will capture your imagination and, we hope, make you a devotee of what are the most wonderful plants in the world—orchids.

# ABOUT ORCHIDS

Orchids are special plants, if for no other reason than the mystique that surrounds them. Stories and fables—true, almost true, and imagined—have grown along with this group of plants since time immemorial. Man has known about and ascribed mystical powers to orchids for as long as history has been written. Over 2,000 years ago, Confucius wrote, in ancient China, about the graceful foliage and delicate fragrance of Cymbidium orchids. Indeed, the Chinese name for orchids, *lan*, signifies perfume and beauty.

The Greeks knew about orchids, too. The name, orchid, is derived from the Greek name for testicles, *orchis*, which the tubers of certain terrestrial orchid species resemble. The plants were thought to grow where animals had spilled their semen on the ground, giving rise to flowers that mimicked the animal. In the medieval belief of the Doctrine of Signatures (where plant and animal parts act upon the portions of the human body that they most resemble), tubers of *Orchis* species were thought to confer virility and potency when consumed. We can only conjecture whether orchids were part of the Hanging Gardens of Babylon, or to what esoteric decorative purpose Asiatic potentates may have put them. We do know, however, that orchid plants did not form a significant part of the Western garden palette much before the late 18th century. A part of the pharmacopoeia, certainly, but in the garden, no.

As the Renaissance began to fade and a more practical Age of Reason began to dawn in our Western culture, there was

Above: *Masd. floribunda.*

again the time and the wherewithal for people to contemplate nature in its bounty. The strange beauty of orchid flowers worked their magic on those who would one day be called scientists. Why did some orchid flowers look so much like insects? By what inconceivable means did their tiny, inconsequential seeds ever give rise to plants? These and more questions arose as scientifically-oriented explorers and expeditions ranged farther and farther afield, in search of not just booty, but knowledge of this wide, wide world they suddenly found spread out before them.

Botanical curiosities were the order of the day, as their pharmacology and other economic uses were investigated. The "nature of orchids" was not so easily elucidated, as an increasingly broad range of plants entered our reposi-tory of knowledge, as tropical orchids entering Western thought were not easy to maintain in captivity. Early botanists certainly knew that this bizarre group of highly differing plants were somehow related, but how and why was not readily apparent, and living material was rare in the extreme. As an example, the earliest tropical orchid to flower in England (1731) arrived as a "dried" herbarium specimen. It had sprouted from the seemingly lifeless "bulb" (more on terminology later) during its transit

from Jamaica, and when potted up, grew and flowered. We now know this plant as *Bletia verrucunda*.

This was the beginning of over 200 years of experiment, failure, and success, in the discovery of the botany and horticulture of the diverse Orchidaceae. The growth in interest and enthusiasm in this group of plants closely parallels the rise to dominance of Western culture. This growth is,

Left: *Bletia verecunda*.

of course, simply a by-product of the increasing availability and the economic means to engage in the study of objects of beauty and novelty, and not anything particularly deep or profound. It just is. Nevertheless, our knowledge of orchids as plants and as flowers (as well as objects of beauty and desire) grew at an ever-increasing rate throughout the 20th century and is still progressing in the new millennium. What, then, have we learned?

## What are orchids and what makes them special?

Orchids are one of the many families of flowering plants that are characterized by the most highly evolved method of reproduction in the plant family. Orchids are monocots (as opposed to dicots) and share this trait with palms, grasses, lilies, and aroids (philodendrons and their relatives). The orchid family, the Orchidaceae, is one of the three largest families of flowering plants—the other two are grasses and daisies—with between 25,000 and 35,000 naturally occurring species. Exactly how many species there are, and exactly what constitutes a distinct species, is one of the aspects of the orchid family that makes it so special.

The classical definition of a species is a distinct population of organisms that is reproductively isolated. That is, the members of the population look different from their relatives, and they effectively don't interbreed. The reproductive isolation can take the form of geographic isolation (they are separated by a mountain), seasonal isolation, pollinator isolation (they attract different pollinators), physical isolation (the parts don't fit), or physiological isolation (the parts don't work together). More often than not, it is a combination of these factors, with physiological isolation playing a major role. This has two important ramifications.

In orchids, unlike most other organisms, physiological barriers have not developed against interspecific (between different species of the same genus) or intergeneric (between different, but obviously related, genera) reproduction. This has led to nearly countless manmade hybrids (over

Left: *Blc.* Dora Louise Capen "Lea" (HCC/AOS)

Above: *Onc. (Tolumnia) bahamense*, restricted to a small area of South Florida near West Palm Beach.

100,000 registered by the late 1990s) of perplexing complexity. To cite two examples just within one breeding group: the cattleyas are intergeneric hybrids that can be traced back over twelve generations to the species parents; and there are currently nonageneric (nine genera) intergeneric hybrids! That's right: they are hybrids with nine genera in their background. We'll need to revisit this aspect a little later with discussions that will help you to understand what orchid hybrids names can (and can't) tell you.

While not a particularly recently evolved group of plants, orchids are highly evolved and still rapidly evolving. The hazy nature of the boundaries between closely related species, and (often) their ability to interbreed if the opportunity is presented, makes orchid taxonomy one of the most contentious of all sciences. Orchid populations may be limited to one small valley high in the Andes, with similar but distinct populations in adjacent valleys. Who is to determine when they are separate species? The reverse situation must also be considered. A widespread species, occurring over a broad area, has a range of color forms and flowering season. If flowers from the extremes of the populations are compared, one might easily consider them as distinct. However, a gamut of variation between the two extremes can be demonstrated. This issue will be explored later, when we discuss the collector and the importance of having something perceived as unique.

Orchids, then, are flowering plants in the monocot group. They share a collection of characters with other members of this large group, including parallel venation of leaves and tripartite floral structure. However, it is in the floral structure that orchids show their truly special nature. Like their relatives, the lilies, orchid flowers are formed of two whorls of three parts. The outer whorl are known as sepals, and the inner whorl as petals, with one of the petals usually modified into a pollinator-attractive structure known as the lip. The lip serves to induce pollinators to interact (unintentionally on the part of the pollinator, of course) with the orchid's uniquely joined sexual structure, the column. The male part the anther, is joined in the same structure with the female organ, the stigma. The male structures are almost always positioned so that the pollinator does not pick up the particular flower's pollinia until after it has deposited previously attached pollinia on the stigmatic surface, which is most often positioned behind (toward the

Left: *Spath. plicata* and *Masd. floribunda* (see page 10) are very widespread and opportunistic orchids.

ovary) the anther. It is this mechanism, coupled with the astonishing ability of orchids to rapidly adapt to new conditions, that has led to some of nature's closest and most bizarre relationships between pollinator and flower.

Color—sometimes invisible to the human eye—is, of course, one of the principal methods of attraction, but other means cannot be overlooked, as orchids employ them all, vigorously, to ensure their fertilization. Flower shape, as noted above, can often resemble the pollinator, triggering either a mating or combative response; or it can mimic other flowers in the vicinity which pollinators are accustomed to visiting. Scent—often not perceptible to the human sense of smell—plays a major role in the attraction of pollinators, and many times at rates that are so low as to be incredible. This method has the largest range of all attractants, and operates at the molecular level. Whether promising nectar or sex, scent is a powerful method of attraction. When taken as a gestalt, the lure

Left: This close-up shot shows the relationship between the column and the lip, with the anther cap tipping the column.

Above: An even closer shot demonstrates the brightly colored area that serves to mark the "landing platform" for pollinators.

of orchid flowers is clearly powerful, as can be seen by the photographs in this book.

Which animals pollinate orchids? Bats, bees, butterflies, moths, birds, mosquitoes, gnats, and humans. What happens when an orchid flower is pollinated? A seedpod, sometimes called a bean in honor of the vanilla beans of commerce, forms containing thousands to hundreds of thousands of tiny, dust-like seeds. This fecund habit has some important particulars. First, so many seeds imply an equal or greater number of embryos needing fertilization by pollen grains. The pollen masses of orchids—held together in a waxy aggregation known as pollinia—ensure that the many needed pollen grains are placed in the right location by the pollinator.

Second, orchid seed is fine and dust-like, with little or none of the starchy endosperm that normally "powers" young seedlings until they are able to produce their own nourishment by photosynthesis. This "bare" seed requires a very specialized relationship with a mycorhizal fungus whose metabolic processes provide the necessary nutrients for the germination and initial growth of the young orchid. Some orchids cannot continue to grow to maturity and beyond without these mycorhizal fungi, which invade the orchid seed through a precise area of the seedcoat. Therefore, the production of thousands of seeds ensures that at least a few will be windborne to a spot where the vital fungus grows. Clearly, such a hit-or-miss, low probability method of propagation, has real drawbacks for commercial production.

Above: *Pot.* Twentyfour Carat "Lea" (AM/AOS)

## How do orchids grow?

The first obstacle to be overcome by orchid growers in the early years of the hobby was the common misconception of the conditions under which tropical plants grow in the wild. The jungle was thought to be much like what we imagine when we think of Tarzan films, or Humphrey Bogart traveling down river in *The African Queen*: hot, sticky, and shady. (And so it is at sea level, along rivers and watercourses where light can penetrate to the ground, but this is not prime orchid habitat.) Early growers sought to emulate these conditions in structures aptly named "stoves," where the temperature was kept elevated by coal heaters, the humidity kept high by continual "damping down" (the process of wetting

Above: *Den. crumenatum*, whose flowers open for only a few hours after a cooling rainstorm, have a strong scent to lure their pollinator.

Right: *Bulb. graveolens* with fly pollinator. Many orchids have fetid odors that attract flies and other carrion-loving insects.

Above: *Brassia pumila*. Some members of this genus have patterns that are only visible with UV light and mimic a spider in its web. A parasitic wasp attacks what it thinks is the spider, pollinating the flower.

walkways and benches), and the light level was kept low by painted glass. Any form of air circulation was considered a "no-no." Under these harsh conditions, England became what was known as the "graveyard of tropical plants." Orchids and other exotics already suffering from weeks or months in transit were potted in rotting wood and thrust into the hot and sticky confines of a stove. They would occasionally flower, to great fanfare, only to decline and perish. No wonder. Nothing could be further from the environment typically enjoyed by many of the most commonly imported orchids than that of a stove.

Many of our most commonly cultivated orchids come from areas where they get strong light, dappled by a light canopy of foliage, continual air movement, moderate, but not stifling, humidity, and periods of wet and dry conditions, as the passing showers alternate with the sun. Many orchids come from areas of seasonal dryness and cooler temperatures, often from higher elevations in the foothills of tropical areas, where the temperature regime resembles that further away from the Equator. Bright, airy, and comfortable: what could be further from the stoves of Victorian England?

Early collectors were not eager to dispel these myths, either, as it would have served both to unlock the secrets of the habitats where they collected the plants, as well as reduce their market if fewer plants died. Nevertheless, as more information slowly emerged about the increasingly less mysterious tropical and subtropical areas, thoughtful gardeners began to experiment with other cultural treatments. Men like Joseph Paxton (later Sir Joseph as a result of his pioneering efforts with orchids), gardener to our friend, the "Bachelor Duke" of Devonshire, began to explore the possibilities of admitting air and light to the oppressive stoves, with astounding effects. The result was an explosion in the successful cultivation of a wide variety of orchid plants once thought to be impossible. An attendant explosion in the number of successfully cultivated orchid species led to

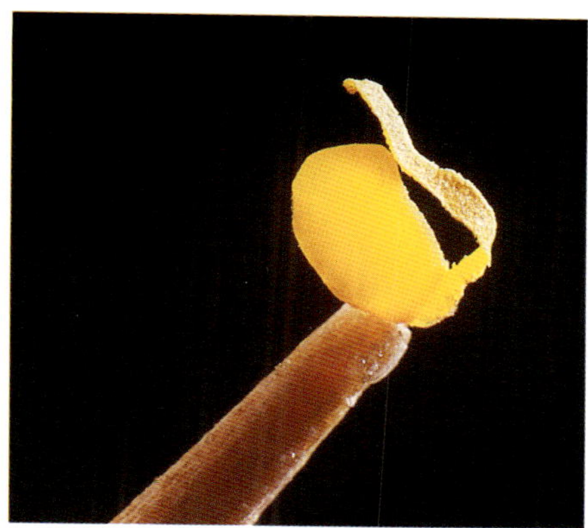

Above: Pollen mass, on the tip of a toothpick.

Above: Close-up of orchid seedlings growing on agar medium in seedling flask. These plants are about 18 months old from seed!

vast growth in the knowledge about them.

One of the primary mysteries concerned the pollination of orchids and the subsequent germination of their tiny seeds. Orchids are not pollinated like other "flowers," nor does the seed respond like "other seed." Orchids mystified these pioneering horticulturists. How were the flowers made to form seedpods—which were occasionally present on freshly imported plants—and what factors were involved with the germination of the dust-like seed? While research on pollination biology would have to wait, horticulturists began to understand how to pollinate orchids by the mid-18th century. They did not, however, have any understanding as to how the seed itself germinated, or how to maintain what few seedlings they might accidentally obtain as "volunteers" on the roots of freshly imported specimens.

Above: A ripe orchid seed pod, showing the fine, dustlike seed.

Some limited success was gained by sowing the seed around the base of the mother plant—the plant from which the seed was obtained—or around the base of another established plant. It should be noted here that these plants had all been wild-collected, so whatever mysterious property enabled seed to germinate and the plants to grow must have been present. With luck—or good care—a few of the seeds would germinate into what are now known as protocorms, when they would be "pricked off" the mother plant (or sometimes just left to grow on) and put into small, community pots, which could then be cultured under more exacting conditions than those demanded by the mature plants. In nature, of course, the seedlings grew where they fell, and often under the same conditions that they would grow for the duration of their lives, excepting, of course, when the forest environment changed.

Right: *Sobralia decora* growing in situ in Central America. This is a widespread terrestrial genus.

As both orchid culture and the supporting scientific technology became more sophisticated, the wealthy few orchid hobbyists gave financial support to research to discover how and why orchid seed germinated. In 1899, with the help of increasingly fine microscopy, Noel Bernard demonstrated the germination of wild orchid seed in the presence of a mycorhizal fungus. By culturing the fungus and obtaining a "pure culture," the symbiotic method of seed germination was developed, though this method was not widely used by an industry still in its infancy. The method, while effective, was relatively complex owing to the time-consuming process needed to obtain the proper fungal isolate for seed inoculation. As a side note, the symbiotic method of seed germination is again becoming relevant in the production of otherwise-intractable temperate-zone terrestrials.

Further research into this orchid

Left: *Enc. tampensis* growing in situ in its Florida habitat, increasingly endangered by encroaching development and collecting. Typical epiphytic habit.

seed-fungal relationship led to the discovery by Hans Burgeff in 1908 that orchid seed would germinate *in vitro* (under artificial conditions) in the presence of the mycorhizal fungi and that the fungi converted starch into sugar, the nutrients needed by the developing orchid embryo. Finally, in 1921, Dr. Lewis Knudson published his pioneering paper outlining his nutrient media for the asymbiotic germination of orchid seed and an industry was born. The means for propagating orchids by the tens and hundreds of thousands had been discovered, and a flurry of hybridizing quickly and inevitably followed.

## Where do they grow?

No basic outline of orchids would be complete without a discussion of the many ecological niches inhabited by this versatile and opportunistic group of plants. In answer to the question "Where do orchids grow?" the simple answer would have to be "Just about everywhere." Orchids are found from just below the Arctic Circle nearly to the Antarctic Circle; from sea level to over 12,000ft; in trees, on rocks, in sand, soil, forest duff and even underground; in jungles, forests, deserts, mountains, prairies, and swamps. Just about everywhere.

More importantly, though, than their diversity of habitat, is what is represented by their adaptability. While many orchids are versatile in a way that enables them to quickly invade disrupted habitats, some are not. Some orchids have very little tolerance for change in their environment or have specific and elaborate relationships with their pollinators that prevent them from spreading beyond a very closely defined niche. It is these orchids that are becoming the pandas of the plant family, representative of the need to preserve habitats of high biodiversity as resources for the future. Where such orchids occur are often the richest and most diverse habitats on the planet. If people and their governments can be convinced that habitats of rare and exotic orchids must be preserved, these same habitats will be able to continue to harbor the rest of the rich flora and fauna they contain.

How, though, do the habitat preferences

Right: *Dresslerella pilossisima*, a hairy miniature *pleurothallid*.

of the species progenitors of our most commonly grown orchids influence their culture? As already noted, most of our best-loved orchids come from the low to middle elevations of the tropics and subtropics, where they grow as epiphytes (using trees as support to reach for light and more nutrient-rich areas) or forest floor hemi-epiphytes (*on* the forest floor, in humusy duff, rather than *in* the soil).

A little ecology note is justified here. Most forest habitats are incredibly efficient by design. Not a lot of excess nutrients are available in the soil; nearly all is "invested" if you will, in the continuing business of life. For this reason, the forest floor is often an open and nearly sterile environment, with intense competition for whatever light and detritus might eventually reach surface level. Various canopies of vegetation compete vigorously for light and nutrients. Many of our most

Left: *Oeceoclades maculata*—many orchids are extremely opportunistic and might be considered "weeds." This plant emigrated into the US from Asia in grass seed.

popular orchids have evolved to take advantage of an epiphytic habit to grow higher in the canopy where light levels are more favorable and the trapping of detritus gives an increased level of nutrients. Along with these factors come increased air circulation and regular rainfall, owing to both lower water-retentive substrates, and to the seasonality of rain in such environments.

Many other commonly grown plants share this niche. Aroids (philodendrons, spathiphyllums, and anthuriums), gesneriads (African violets and their relatives), begonias, ferns, cacti (Christmas and Easter cactus), and bromeliads are just a few examples. All of these plants are successfully grown in homes around the world. By extension, so can orchids. Good light from a shaded south, east, or west window, plus moderate humidity, and even moisture, are easily provided in most homes. Even better are solariums or other dedicated growing structures, including greenhouses. Just remember the hard lessons learned by our Victorian forerunners, and success with orchids can be yours.

## Who grows them?

As discussed above, orchids started as a hobby of the elite, who could afford to obtain and then maintain them. Secondarily, of course, came those who were in the employ of—directly or indirectly—this elite. Orchids were, simply put, expensive. Even today's most egalitarian group, the American Orchid Society (AOS)—whose recent presidents have included a retired school teacher, a working wife, a realtor, a retired executive, and an insurance agent—was formed by a group in the northeastern United States consisting of wealthy amateurs and the men (yes, men, only one woman was included in the 100 charter members) who provided their orchids.

Knudson's formula provided the breakthrough in production technology that made orchids available to the less affluent middle class. When it became feasible to raise thousands upon thousands of plants—hybrid or species—from seed, easily and relatively cost-effectively, prices of orchids fell to the point where they were accessible to this quickly growing class. Indeed, it became vitally necessary to exploit this growing market to place the many plants

that were being produced and to continue to generate the revenue that drove the fledgling industry.

Immediately after World War 2, as leisure time and expendable income became the order of the day, hobbies came to be a major industry in the United States. A necessity of the lean war years that carried over into post-war culture was gardening. Growing vegetables gave way to flower gardening, flower gardening grew into the desire to obtain and grow the more unusual and exotic tropicals that were being seen at flower shows. As more orchids were sold, increasing numbers of people became interested in trying to make a "go" of orchids as a business. "Mom and Pop" nurseries, supplying the expanding market, sprung up in nearly every affluent, and some not-so-affluent, community. Larger nurseries put out elaborate catalogs designed to capture the imaginations of the newcomers, and, not coincidentally, their purchasing dollars. The orchid industry, while remaining rather specialized, continued to grow well into the 1970s, especially with the advent of cloning.

Local orchid societies proliferated, serving more and more specific communities within the larger metropolitan areas. For example, the Joint Presidents Council is a group of local presidents from societies serving the New York metropolitan area. There are currently more than a dozen societies represented in this group. Orchid culture information became more widely spread, and more diverse, as a result of an increasingly broad popular base. The magazine of the AOS, the *Bulletin*, was the "bible" to orchid growers around the U.S. and the AOS judging system was the main arbiter of what constituted a quality orchid. Today, the *Bulletin* is known simply as *Orchids*, and nearly 600 AOS judges perform their tasks internationally, as well as at 29 monthly Center Judgings, with more than 200 orchid shows judged in the course of a typical year.

The AOS is the model orchid society, and all are welcomed, rich, poor, commercial, and amateur. Orchid growing is no longer the pastime of the rich and famous, but a relaxing and enjoyable hobby with

Left: *Catasetum tabulare* in situ in Colombia, another very opportunistic, fast-growing orchid.

plants, especially now that the requisite knowledge to grow them is freely available.

## Economics of orchids

A misunderstood and rarely discussed topic in the field of orchidology pertains to the economics of the hobby and the trade. First, it should be understood that some orchids are better than others. Whether because of intrinsic beauty, relative quality, rarity, or distinction, the best orchids command prices exponentially higher than those of their average siblings. Even in the very earliest days of the hobby, when all plants were wild-collected and sold at auction when not in bloom, certain characteristics would recommend one plant or groups of plants over another, with a resultant price differential. A new introduction? From a different and less accessible location? Larger and more robust plants? Reported to have rounder, fuller segmented, and more colorful blooms? All of these factors contributed to significant price differences.

Left: *Aerides odorata* in situ, with masses of pendant, fragrant blooms, is easily naturalized in frost-free gardens.

Dealers counted on higher prices from the best plants to offset losses in transit, as well as the potential lack of interest in other, more common lots. Buyers counted on getting the rarest and best for their investment, if only for bragging rights. It was well known that, even in the rare cases where seed could be obtained from the best varieties and plants grown, the progeny would not be exactly true to the parent in quality, but rather exhibiting a range of variation. The only way to get a guaranteed "good one" was to buy a division, or propagation, of the exact plant at the price set by the owner. Such prices could soar into the thousands or tens of thousands of dollars, when the plants were sparingly made available. Even today, exclusively held plants, or plants that cannot be cloned (such as paphiopedilums), can command exceptionally high prices—the modern known record is $25,000!

As seed propagation became practical and more widely practiced, prices for average plants began to fall; not precipitously, but slowly. Hybrids became more common, yet the best were still only one in a thousand (or less) and still considered extremely valuable, as they could not be reliably duplicated. Cloning, or meristemming as it came to be known, became a practical reality in the late 1960s. With this process, the result of research by Dr. Georges Morel and Dr. Don Wimber, orchids could be reproduced exactly, reliably, and by the thousands, thereby bringing even the very best varieties within the reach of the masses. This process, ironically, served to initially increase profitability for commercial growers, and later, to depress prices for what had been their most profitable varieties. Price became the competitive point rather than quality of the plant. Today, we see meristems as the basis of a rapidly growing mass-market-driven industry, with overall plant performance the watchword rather than the quality of the bloom.

Today's orchid industry, like perhaps no other period in its history, is highly stratified and suffering not a little from bipolar disease. On one hand we have the traditional orchid nurseries, those that have catered to the specialized hobby trade, and on the

Right: RF Orchids, in Homestead, Florida is typical of a well-kept commercial orchid nursery.

Above: The public flocks to orchid shows around the world, especially the triennial World Orchid Conference, here illustrated when in Rio de Janeiro, Brazil in 1996.

other, the modern mass-market-driven nurseries whose clients are the largest retailers and only secondarily the consumer. Sadly, many of these mass-market nurseries are not even interested in the name of the plants they are growing, their interests lying solely in whether or not the plants grow, flower, and sell quickly.

This is in direct contrast to the traditional orchid-hobbyist market, whose directive from their individual clients was for quality and distinction above all else. Many times, too, these more traditionally oriented growers started out as hobbyists, and only began to sell plants as a way of dealing with the overflow from their burgeoning collections and as a method of earning money to buy more. For this reason, many so-called orchid businesses are not always run with the best idea of true costs and overheads,

## Orchid Judging

The judging of orchid flowers has two important facets: show (or ribbon) judging and quality judging. Show judging can be simply explained as the evaluation of what is the best for its type exhibited on the day. Is it the best (or second-best or third-best) white Cattleya orchid on display here today? Quality judging, on the other hand, is based on criteria developed on a global scale over years of training and experience as to what constitutes a good example of the type and breeding. In other words, is it a good white Cattleya given its parentage?

Many national and international bodies, including the American Orchid Society (AOS), the Royal Horticultural Society (RHS), and the Japan Orchid Growers Association (JOGA), give quality awards. Most often, these awards are based on a 100-point scale, with awards given for grades between 75–79, 80–89, and 90+. In the AOS system, these awards are called the Highly Commended Certificate (HCC/AOS given for 75–79), the Award of Merit (AM/AOS given for 80–89) and the First Class Certificate (FCC/AOS given for 90+). In addition, there is a variety of awards for botanical and cultural recognition.

The AOS gives more than 2,000 awards annually but only a dozen or so FCC/AOS. Flower quality awards are highly coveted and significantly increase the value of an awarded plant. Certified orchid judges often spend years in training to obtain their certification, and are expected to serve without compensation, as well as maintain their certification by continuing education.

rather as a simple means of supporting the habits of the owners. Having an orchid business also serves, in some cases, as a tax dodge, as well as a way of obtaining discounts that may not be warranted simply on volume of purchase.

## Why do we grow them?

There are more orchids available today than at any other time in the history of horticulture, yet membership in orchid societies remains stagnant, if not actually decreasing. A visit to a local orchid society in nearly any city will show a membership highly skewed to older members, with only a few younger—and by younger I mean under 40—members. How to capture a portion of the many orchid purchasers remains a constant topic of discussion among orchid society leadership around the nation. Nevertheless, new orchid growers are being recruited and their demographic profile is not significantly different today than it was 40 or 50 years ago.

What sort of person is attracted to orchid growing as a hobby? Lovers of beauty, certainly. Gardeners who want to be challenged, too. But the slightly arcane and exotic aura of orchids also attracts a goodly number of what can best be called collectors. Yes, the same types who might collect stamps, or cameras, or "Precious Moments," also are drawn to the orchid hobby. They enjoy having something beautiful that no one else has, or that has taken some sacrifice on their part to obtain. Collectors enjoy sharing their accomplishments with other collectors. For this, we can be thankful, for without this sharing the world of orchids would be much poorer. It is the collectors who drive our hobby and support our commercial friends. It is the collectors who form new orchid societies and are the officers of the old groups. It is the collectors who become judges and, often, smaller commercial growers.

We collectors want to share with you our passion for this uniquely beautiful and rewarding group of plants. Join us for a spell. You'll be glad you did.

Right: *Slc.* Hazel Boyd "Elizabeth" (AM/AOS)—a fine example of one of the most highly awarded orchid hybrids of all time, it was considered quite a breakthrough in type when first shown.

# GROWING ORCHIDS AT HOME

Not everyone can have a greenhouse, but just about everyone can grow orchids at home. Pretty tall words. Yet, as discussed in the opening chapter of this book, many people already successfully grow orchid "neighbors," that is, plants that grow right alongside orchids in nature. Anyone who has grown an African violet, or a bromeliad, or a begonia, can surely grow an orchid. All that is required is bright light, whether from a window or from an artificial source, moderate humidity and a willingness to treat the plants with appropriate care. Appropriate care is one of those hard-to-define concepts, rather like in cooking, but, as in cooking, the perceptive grower will quickly learn just how much is enough and how much is too much. And "too much" is worse than "not enough." Too much light, or water, or fertilizer, or any one of a number of factors, will more quickly kill your plants than just slightly too little.

Perhaps the most important aspect of successful orchid growing is good observational skills. Interpreting your observations of the plants' responses to their environment and to your treatment of them will enable you to better provide for their critical needs. First, an analysis of your potential growing area will give you a better idea of what plants may be best suited to the conditions you are able to provide for them. There are many beautiful orchids that will perform satisfactorily under such a variety of conditions that it makes sense to select those that will succeed for you. Once you have some experience, you may want to try more marginal types, but at first, select those that will grow and flower easily in your conditions.

Above: *Phal.* Brother Precious Stones

Second, learn to observe more than the immediately obvious symptom. Just as in a runny nose, which can be caused by a variety of reasons from allergies to a noseful of pepper, so can various orchid symptoms be caused by a variety of ailments. The most common example is dehydration of the leaves, which often causes a leathery appearance, accompanied by a dull, wrinkled texture. Dehydration occurs when the leaves are not getting enough water. Underwatering or overwatering most often causes this. Underwatering is easy to understand and is diagnosed by the pot being quite light with the roots appearing healthy and white. The medium will also appear to be in good condition, and will retain a firm consistency. The grower may have to water the plant several times in succession to rewet the medium, and pay closer attention that the plant does not dry so thoroughly in future.

But how can overwatering cause dehydration? Overwatering can and often does lead to rapid deterioration of the medium with consequent root loss. This condition is diagnosed by the dark and saturated appearance of the medium, a relatively heavy pot and dark, unhealthy roots. The medium will have broken down and will need to be replaced. Unfortunately, this is the more frequently encountered situation and is quite difficult to remedy. Most orchids are seasonal in their rooting behavior; that is, they root only during certain times of the year. If they are potted during a season when they are unlikely to grow new roots, they may suffer more than if

Above: Nothing is more decorative and long lasting in the home than a flowering orchid plant.

Above: Good observation skills are what separate the average grower from the master grower.

kept on the dry side until new rooting is expected.

With these few examples in mind, let's go on to the particular needs of the plants and relate those needs to potential problem areas. We won't discuss temperature beyond a few generalities in each section, as the temperature of your home is what it is, that with which you are comfortable and is appropriate to your climate. Part of your observational duties are to determine your general temperature regime, and obtain plants that are appropriate to that regime, based on the information given earlier for each group.

## Light

This is the single most critical factor in the successful culture of orchids. If you are already growing a few, and your plants are not flowering, the chances are pretty good that they are not getting enough light. How much is enough is, of course, dependent on the particular orchid. However, in the home, the prevailing wisdom is that a lightly shaded south window is best, followed closely by an east window (plants love

Above: Desiccated, leathery leaves are a symptom of dehydration, most often caused by root loss.

Above: Rotted roots appear black, squishy, and generally dead.

morning sun in the same way people do), and lastly by a west window. (Light and heat are related, and for this reason, a west window often gives light that is too hot for good orchid growing.) Very seldom will a north window provide enough quality light to flower orchids.

Light quality is an important concept to understand. The quality of light coming through any window is already less than that of light that comes from directly overhead, as in a greenhouse or sunroom, simply because it is incidental, or angled, light. Such light is of lower energy, hence quality, than overhead light. This is why a southern window is best, as it will allow light into the growing area with the least diminution of quality. Summer light is better than winter light for the very same reason. The sun is at a higher angle—more overhead—in summer than in winter. In the home, the more the grower can do to maximize light quality, the better his or her plants will do, and the greater the selection of plants the grower will be able to master.

In general, quantity of light will not make up for quality. More—longer hours—of poor quality light will not be the same. Indeed, increasing day length beyond a certain point will actually be detrimental to the health and flowering of your plants, as orchids need darkness to complete their metabolic processes. Never allow your plants more than 16 hours of light per day.

Above: The plant on the left has had adequate light as evidenced by its naturally upright growth and good flower production, while the plant on the right shows the effects of poor light by the dark green color and lack of flowers.

It is perfectly acceptable, and, indeed, necessary in many cases, to enhance available light with artificial sources. Such sources can range from the straightforward four-tube florescent set-up to HID lights. The use of artificial lighting, whether to supplement available light or as a substitute, will enable the grower to greatly expand the range of plants with which they can succeed.

Too little light will result in weak plants that will not flower regularly, if at all. The most obvious symptoms are soft, dark green foliage, spindly pseudobulbs unable to support their own weight, most often accompanied by the diminishing size of pseudobulbs or foliage, and the premature loss of lower or older leaves. An increased susceptibility to disease is often found as well. Too much light will more rarely be a problem except at the change of seasons from winter into spring, where rapidly changing light conditions can lead to sunburn symptoms, or when a plant is too quickly moved from a lower into a higher light situation. Both of these scenarios can be likened to your first day at the beach after a long winter. Your skin simply isn't used to the higher levels of sunlight and is more subject to burning when too quickly exposed, while if given increasing levels and lengths of exposure, your skin—and the plant's leaves—can properly adjust. Especially in more northern areas, as the sun's angle rises in the sky with the approach of spring, it is imperative to watch your plants closely to ensure that they don't accidentally get more light than they can handle.

What we call sunburn is not directly caused by the sun, either, but as a result of heat buildup from the sun's rays. For this reason, you will see the symptoms of burning on the flat part of the leaf that is most exposed to the sun. This will start as a

Above: Sunburn is a misnomer, as it is the heat of the sun and not the sun itself that causes symptoms such as this. Plants left in the car on a sunny day can quickly burn, even if parked in the shade.

lighter colored area and progress rapidly to black, followed by a dead brown central area ringed with black. The best guard against this occurrence is to make sure that your growing area has some provision for temporary shading—light cheesecloth is an excellent temporary measure—along with good air circulation to prevent heat buildup. Otherwise, strong light is good for your plants!

A last good trick to remember is to summer your plants out-of-doors on a shaded patio or lanai, if possible. They will show their appreciation by improved growth and flowering. Remember to give them acclimatization time when first moving them into the higher light regime of out-of-doors.

## Humidity (and air circulation)

The second crucial factor in successful home orchid culture is the maintenance of adequate humidity. It is also nearly as fraught with difficulty as trying to obtain the correct light levels, owing to a sort of "Catch 22." Orchid plants grow best with humidity in the 40%–60% rh range. (Rh or "relative humidity" is defined as the amount of water held by a volume of air compared to the amount it could potentially hold. The potential water-holding capacity of air rises with temperature. Therefore, a volume of air with a fixed amount of moisture will have an rh that is inversely proportional to the temperature of the air. Plants prefer the opposite: rh should rise with temperature, so water needs to be added to the air as it warms.) Unfortunately, not only is this range sometimes a little uncomfortable for

Below: Good air circulation is a must for successful orchid culture.

people but the furniture, the drapes, the rugs, and the "vac" all conspire to rob the air of its moisture.

Home growers can maintain adequate humidity by a variety of means. The least effective is the most popular: misting does very little good except for the grower. It is far more important to raise the humidity in the general area of the plants and the most effective way of doing this is to grow the plants in groups. Placing groups of plants together allows them to take advantage of their collective transpiration to create a more favorable microclimate.

Another important way that humidity is controlled is through the admission of fresh, moving air whenever possible. Except on the very coldest days, the window near which the plants are growing should be partially opened to allow the circulation of fresh air. Stagnant air allows the buildup of pathogens that can cause many of the more common fungal and bacterial ailments that affect orchids. A light movement of air through the growing area will help to prevent such problems, as well as keeping temperatures even throughout the area.

## Watering

Watering and humidity are, of course, intimately related—and we all love to water, don't we? Mastering the water needs of your orchid plants is the closest you can come to controlling their destiny. As many experienced growers are fond of saying, "who holds the hose, grows the rose." This applies to orchids, too. Novice growers want to know: "How often should I water?" The correct answer is: "Water when the plants need it." This fails to satisfy. Most orchids will do best if watered before becoming completely dry. Allowing plants to dry too thoroughly has several affects, including over-concentration of soil salt solution and attendant root problems, as well as making the medium much more difficult to rewet.

A word of explanation here might help. Orchid media are made up of various materials that naturally hold by gravity varying degrees of water. This same force will also hold air. Most media are designed to hold some air and some water, to allow for the gas exchange so necessary to orchid roots. The water that is held in the medium contains a solution (the "soil solution") of

Above: A bamboo skewer makes a good way to test for moisture content of the media: if it comes up dark, there is enough water; if light, it needs water.

various salts. This is concentrated as the roots take up water at a higher rate. Once the soil solution reaches a certain concentration of salinity, it becomes toxic to the roots. Also, as the soil solution disappears, the medium holds more air, and this air becomes more difficult to displace. When you water a plant and the water appears to "run right through" without getting the medium wet, this is what has happened. Watering several times in succession, or sitting the pot in a saucer of water until the medium has "rewet" is the solution here. So, don't let your plants get as dry as the desert; rather water them before they are completely dry.

The particular watering needs of any

Right: Watering is the best time to really look over your plants to see how they are growing, and to catch any potential problems before they get a hold. "Who holds the hose, grows the rose."

orchid will depend on that plant. Phalaenopsis and paphiopedilums prefer to be evenly moist, while cattleyas like to approach dryness and oncidiums like to be somewhere in the middle. Phragmipediums, unlike almost every other type of plant, actually like to sit in water, as long as it is changed every so often. The watering needs of dendrobiums will depend on the type. Many times, your developing observational powers will help you to identify a plant's watering needs, by how quickly the plant dries between waterings. If it seems to dry quickly, water it more frequently. It is that simple. This will also help you to know whether a plant may be resting during winter months. If it doesn't seem to be drying during what have come to be its regular watering intervals, just hold off and let it dry.

Above: *C. walkeriana* shows a typical sympodial mode of growth, climbing up a tree branch.

Above: A vanda shows monopodial, upright, growth.

## Potting and potting media

Your choice of potting media should be governed by four conventional factors: availability, utility, reproducibility, and cost. In other words: Can you get it? Does it work? It is of uniform quality? Can you

Above: There are a variety of potting media available today. Clockwise from top of photo: Tree fern fiber, rockwool, osmunda, sphagnum moss, Aliflor, lava rock, and fir bark in center.

afford it? In the home, a potting medium needs to be water-retentive, yet drain freely and dry at a uniform rate. The supply and quality of fir bark, once ubiquitous, has declined to a point where it is no longer so generally used. Today, you are just as liable to see orchids grown in what would once have been seen as "house plant" potting soil, as you might in rock, or in sphagnum moss.

Truth be told, orchids will grow equally well in a variety of materials, as long as watering and fertilizing are adjusted appropriately. Also, your general climatic area will dictate your choice, especially if you intend to summer your plants out-of-doors. Dry areas will require a more water-retentive, and finer textured, medium; while areas enjoying summer rains will want a coarser, faster-drying mix. Only in the most favorable home conditions will mounting be an option. Mounted orchids require much closer attention to watering and humidity, making this method generally impractical except in the greenhouse. The open basket culture preferred by many vandaceous types falls into this category as well, though with the addition of fast-draining medium, home culture is often successful.

The single most important bit of advice on potting is to pot only when new roots are expected. While rooting occurs in various orchids at various times during their growth cycle, one can never go wrong potting in the spring months. When an orchid is potted at the right time and new roots have the opportunity to grow into fresh media, you have a happy plant. A good rule of thumb is to get your potting done during lengthening days or at least between the equinoxes.

## Fertilizing

Your choice of fertilizer will be governed by your choice of potting medium. Traditional mixes, based on wood products such as fir bark, require high nitrogen fertilizers, while most other media do best when fertilized with a balanced formula. You will see a series of three numbers on fertilizer packaging, known as the N-P-K (nitrogen–phosphate–potassium) ratio. Fertilizers for

Above: Always measure your fertilizer carefully, as overfeeding can lead to poor flowering.

fir bark generally have a 3:1:1 ratio, while a balanced fertilizer will be 1:1:1. If in doubt, use a balanced fertilizer.

A good general rule for fertilizing is "weakly, weekly." Fertilize your plants at approximately one quarter label strength every week, and you'll never have to worry about whether you ought to fertilize this week or not. Your plants will also perform better than with occasional jolts of full strength. Fertilizing and watering go hand-in-hand. If you are watering less frequently, fertilize less. If you are having to water more often, as you may in summer months, you can increase fertilizer commensurately.

## Pests and diseases

Orchids are susceptible to the same sucking pests as other ornamental plants. These pests may be controlled by the same methods, as well. Your choice of method is up to your particular circumstances, whether or not you feel comfortable using the more toxic pesticides that are generally more effective, or prefer to first use some of the less intrusive modern alternatives such as insecticidal soaps or fine horticultural oils.

Above: Mealybugs are one of the most commonly encountered orchid pests and can be controlled with a variety of methods, especially if detected early.

Alcohol and a q-tip work for mild infestations. If you continually practice good observational skills with your plants, and only purchase clean plants to begin with, you'll find that you can contain mild infestations easily and early, and not have to resort to more toxic measures. The most important thing to remember, though, is that one treatment is never enough. You'll need to treat at least twice and often three times, at seven to ten day intervals, to achieve real control.

The most commonly encountered disease problems in orchids are either fungal or bacterial, and both are the result of cultural problems. Such problems are often

Above: Growers in frost-free areas can grow a broad and diverse collection with just a shadehouse, as shown here.

caused by overcrowding, overwatering, or poor sanitation. Too many plants, too much water, or too much debris in the growing area will almost always lead to rot of some kind. If these problems are successfully addressed, the diseases will often naturally and spontaneously be "cured," as long as the diseased parts are removed entirely. The only measure you may have to take is

Above: *Slc.* ewel Box "Scherezade" (AM/AOS)

the occasional use of a material like Physan or RD20 to clean up; otherwise good culture will prevent most disease.

## Some suggestions

Orchid growing is like cooking. No single cookbook is going to teach you how to cook, and no one cook is going to have all of the right answers for your questions. Nor will you ever learn to cook without cooking. The methods and materials, the hints and hindrances given in a variety of sources should be taken as suggestions, as guides along the way. With experience, you will find your own way to grow orchids. It may be ike your neighbor's and it may not. You may feel the urge to experiment, and you should, with one or a few expendable plants, never with all. Above all else, observe and learn, and never lose the sense of joy and accomplishment that a well-grown orchid, flowered by you, can give.

# Potting a Cattleya

The preferred time to repot a sympodial orchid is when there is a cluster of root tips at the base of the new lead. This usually occurs in the spring.

If the orchid is not severely overgrown you can easily remove it from its old pot.

Select a new container that will allow for about two year's additional growth. Add about half an inch to an inch drainage material for a 4–6 inch pot.

Try not to block any of the holes in such a way that would prevent water from escaping.

Place the plant with the oldest part against the rim of the pot and the rhizome half to three-quarters of an inch below the edge. Begin adding the potting media of your choice, here we are using lava rock. You may need to push the media in to the pot depending on what you are using.

Continue to add potting media until it reaches the bottom of the rhizome. Do not cover the rhizome with media. Remove any excess material to where the surface is level and about half to three-quarters of an inch below the edge of the pot

An adult cattleya should be able to be secured with a single rhizome clip if properly placed. If necessary use a straight or ring stake for additional support.

The plant must be firmly anchored or else it will not be able to establish itself.

Prepare a nametag with the name of the orchid, any award and, if you wish, the parentage and date of repotting.

Insert into the pot or use a tie-on tag to tie onto a pseudobulb.

...and that is all there is to it, you're done!

Right: *Lc.* Rojo. Healthy orchids, like this example, reliably produce beautiful blooms for you to enjoy.

# CATTLEYA

When lay people visualize an orchid, the chances are pretty good that what they'll see in their mind's eye is a *Cattleya*—the "Queen of orchids." What could be more emblematic of the Orchidaceae? Frilly, full of form, fragrant, and just plain fantastic, *Cattleyas* epitomize the family. Indeed, the color "orchid" represents the bold rose-purple flower so well remembered by generations of Prom goers. An orchid corsage still conjures visions of luxury and heavenly perfume. Yet, the *Cattleya* that started it all first entered cultivation as packing material! *Cattleya labiata*, the "type specimen" of the genus, came into England around 1810 as packing material around other exotic plants being shipped from the Rio de Janeiro region of Brazil. Yes, there were other *Cattleya*s known to cultivation at the time, notably *C. loddigesii*, but in these early days of orchids, they were still known in a generic sense as *Epidendrum*. Before the true breadth and width of the orchid family became known, most, if not all, of the epiphytic plants were known as "*Epidendrum*," which literally means "on a tree."

However, with the flowering of this plant in 1818, a new genus was declared by John Lindley, *Cattleya*, named after William Cattley, a noted patron of botany. It is difficult to imagine, today, the sensation caused by such a flower. Modern commentators have rightly termed such events and their

Above: *C. Brabantiae* was one of the earliest artificial orchid hybrids and has been remade many times over the last 100 years.

Right: *C. labiata* is the prototypical "orchid" in many people's eyes.

Below: *C. granulosa* "John Jensen" is a good example of this fairly uncommon bifoliate species.

effect "the shock of the new." And shocking indeed was *Cattleya labiata autumnalis vera* ("the true fall-flowering *Cattleya*"). Big, beautiful, and boldly colored with a hue not previously seen, this flower remains one of the most beautiful of the entire family. However, what had entered cultivation as something of much less than significant value—indeed, as material that would cost money to dispose of—now was one of the most valued and sought-after of all plants.

Despite its value and desirability, *C. labiata* was soon lost from cultivation to become an almost mythical Grail-like object of every plant collector's search. *C. labiata* disappeared, like so many other one-time orchid discoveries of the early days, because they simply weren't very good at growing and nobody knew how to look after them properly. Joseph Paxton's breakthroughs in culture were still years in the future, and many orchids, after their initial flowering in cultivation and subsequent botanical description, perished.

This unfortunate situation was exacerbated by several other factors. First and foremost, in the case of *C. labiata*, was that its collection was incidental to the other plants with which it was wrapped. No record was taken of just where—exactly—it had been collected. Second, even when notice was taken of where a particular plant grew, maps were poor in the extreme, and, bluntly, collectors were equivocal in their disclosure of true locations. In addition, entire regions would often be stripped of a desirable plant to maximize the chances of a few surviving the long voyage home, and to preclude any competitors finding the same species for exploitation. In other words, ignorance, greed, and a competitive spirit conspired to make orchid plants and knowledge about them hard-won indeed.

The search for *C. labiata* produced some unexpected results. We can thank this decades-long hunt for the discovery of many of the other labiate-type *Cattleyas*. Several other species were brought into England as the long lost *Cattleya*, only to turn out to be *C. mossiae*, or *C. trianaei*, or *C. mendelii*. All beautiful and worthwhile, but not *C. labiata*. Other *Cattleyas*, *Laelias*, *Brassavolas* and a variety of related genera were also collected and described for the first time during this period, of course, but the search still centered on the most beautiful of all, the true fall-flowering *Cattleya*—*C. labiata*.

Its rediscovery came nearly 20 years later, but the original habitat was found to have been converted to coffee production. A nearby, similar environment was found to contain the plants, but this habitat, too, faced destruction. Thereafter, for nearly 50 years, only illustrations remained to remind history of this wonderful orchid. Once the right niche was refound near Pernambuco, *C. labiata* came to be one of the most commonly grown of all *Cattleyas*, readily and freely available to form the nucleus of a growing cut-flower industry. Today, we know that, in general, *Cattleyas* are among the most widespread and adaptable of all New World orchids.

Perhaps a bit of clarification is in order here. To this point, we've been talking about "true" *Cattleyas*, actual members of

## Some of the most commonly named color types

**Forma typica** — The "typical" color, for example, lavender in labiate, or unifoliate, *Cattleyas*.

**Alba** — Lacking anthocyanin (red or purple) pigment, may be white or green depending on species, breeds true.

**Albescens, or album** — Appearing white, but with some anthocyanin present, breeds colored progeny.

**Semi-alba** — White with a normally colored lip, literally "half white."

**Aquinii** — Peloric, or with petals that closely match the lip pattern and/or shape.

**Coerulea** — "Blue" or cyanotic, as true blue pigments do not exist in *Cattleyas*. The lay person often calls this lavender.

**Flava** — Yellow

There are many other, less well-known, descriptive names used to connote particular color phases, but these are seldom seen outside of orchid specialist circles.

the genus *Cattleya*. From this point on, we'll be using the term to describe a group of plants, all related, whose species have contributed to the modern horticultural type we know as "*Cattleyas*." Species from a variety of genera, as well as hybrids, both simple and complex, make up this group. Because *Cattleyas* (and their relatives) are so widespread and occupy such a variety of habitats, we can infer several important ramifications for their culture. In general, all will grow under the same conditions. We'll discuss this later, but, for now, know that the phrase "grow like a *Cattleya*, but . . ." is one you will hear time and again.

The extraordinarily broad range of colors and shapes has given the hybridizer a palette with which to work that is nearly unequaled in the plant kingdom. And beyond the broad range available between different species and genera, there is often a range of colors available within each species that enables each particular hybrid to have different color forms depending on the parents used. Within the genus *Cattleya* itself, and often with related genera such as *Laelia* and *Sophronitis*, any particular species may have several color phases arising from population isolation in different portions of its range. Such color phases may or may not be accompanied by aberrant growth habits (just like Hillbillies or the Hapsburgs, inbreeding has its benefits and its price), but the color phase will usually breed true when crossed with others of like phase.

The first recorded orchid hybrid—not the first to flower, but the first to be made—was *C. Hybrida*, which was later inferred to be a cross of *C. loddigesii* with *C. guttata*. Inferred, because record keeping was poor and inexact. From that point, in the 1850s, progress was initially slow, until seed-raising techniques improved with practice. Enthusiasm was high, though, for this wonderful group of plants, especially in the unifoliate, larger-flowered types, which were only surpassed by paphiopedilums in the number of hybrids being made and flowered. Considering the variety of colors available even within each species, the range of season—which spreads through

Left: *C. walkeriana* has become one of the most important species parents in modern use. It imparts good size and full shape on small plants, as well as allowing a variety of colors to emerge.

the year—and the showy quality of just about any *Cattleya* flower, it is easy to see why breeders were so eager to create new forms within this malleable group.

As hybridization progressed in this group, and knowledge of habitats increased, it became obvious that some of the plants being imported represented natural hybrids. Indeed, some of the showiest and most popular plants were natural hybrids, formed where species and pollinators overlapped. Growers proved the hybrid nature of these plants by remaking them in cultivation. Two in particular deserve special mention.

*C. dowiana* and *C. warscewiczii* (a.k.a. *C. gigas*) originate in adjacent and often overlapping areas of Colombia. When a brilliantly colored example of what had been imported as *C. warscewiczii* flowered, exhibiting the distinct yellow markings in the throat that characterize *C. dowiana*, a hybrid origin was suspected. These hybrid plants (or those suspected of being such) became highly prized. The London auctions selling imported plants became the scene of spirited bidding for the largest clumps imported as *C. warscewiczii* on the chance that they might be *C. Hardyana*. Of course, the hybrid was also remade artificially; not only confirming the true parents, but also providing a race of brilliantly colored summer-blooming *Cattleyas*.

Interestingly enough, C. *Hardyana* can come in a variety of colors owing to several factors peculiar to *Cattleya* breeding. First, because *Cattleya* species can interbreed in nature where their boundaries overlap, and because such hybrids are themselves often fertile—forming relatively stable populations of their own—what is known as introgressive hybridization is often seen. This means that the hybrids breed among themselves, or back to either parent, forming colonies of plants that may more closely resemble either parent, or larger than expected groups of the primary hybrid. Also, as noted above, *Cattleya* species may come in a variety of color phases. This has resulted in semi-alba (or white with colored lip) forms of *C. Hardyana*, as well as artificially produced light yellow with dark

Right: *C. warscewiczii*, or gigas, is one of the largest of all *Cattleya* flowers, and can reach over nine inches on a mature plant. It flowers in summer and is an important component of lavender *Cattleya* breeding.

lip *C. Hardyanas* resulting from artificially produced sibling crosses.

These light yellow *C. Hardyana* illustrate an important feature of *Cattleya* breeding that was first seen with the production of *C. Fabia* (*labiata x dowiana*). Basically, lavender is dominant over yellow in the breeding of most labiate, or unifoliate ("single leaf" about which more later), *Cattleyas*. In other words, when you cross the yellow *C. dowiana* with the lavender *C. labiata* (or *C. warscewiczii*, for that matter) you get more lavenders. The lavender color is often enhanced by the underlying yellow pigment, but the flowers are lavender, nonetheless. However, in an illustration of Mendellian assortment, if two *C. Fabia* (or two *C. Hardyana*) are crossed together, roughly one quarter of the progeny will exhibit yellow coloration in the classic 1:2:1 ratio. The challenge here is to obtain the desired yellow coloration while also gaining the greater vigor of the *C. labiata* over the *C. dowiana*. Not an easy task!

Left: *C. loddigesii* was one of the first *Cattleyas* to be raised in England and remains a desirable and important species.

This sort of breeding—crossing yellow with lavender—is also where we get the very darkest purple flowers. As mentioned earlier, when yellow and lavender pigments are combined, some percentage of the progeny will have deeper, richer color as a result. The continued breeding in this line results in flowers that approach shades of deep burgundy. However, the challenge remains to select for flower color and form without sacrificing plant vigor.

Today's best known natural hybrid in the genus is *C. Guatemalensis* (*skinneri x aurantiaca*). The combination of the relatively open lavender flower of *C. skinneri* with the more forward-held orange *C. aurantiaca* results, as might be expected, in a bloom intermediate in form and carriage with a broad range of color from rose lavender through salmon to shades of orange and yellow. The plants of *C. skinneri*, *C. aurantiaca*, and *C. Guatemalensis* all look quite similar, especially to the untrained eye and all inhabit similar environments in Central America, especially Guatemala. *C. Guatemalensis* provides a nearly textbook illustration of several of the principles discussed so far, particularly introgressive hybridization in nature. The key factor illustrating the presence of such activity is the range of colors and shapes within the group of plants we recognize as "*C. Guatemalensis*"—because what we know as such is often not really "just" a precise hybrid of a particular *C. skinneri* that has been pollinated by a particular *C. aurantiaca* (or vice versa). What we see are more often members of "hybrid swarms," that is, groups of plants that have resulted from naturally produced hybrids of *C. Guatemalensis* crossed with another *C. Guatemalensis*, or with a *C. skinneri*, or with a *C. aurantiaca* and so on and so on.

The wide range of color within such a group is the first sign of its mixed heritage. Strictly speaking, "true" *C. Guatemalensis*

Left: *C. bicolor*, from Brazil, can be one of the tallest bifoliate *Cattleyas*, reaching over four feet tall on well-grown plants.

Above: *C. skinneri* is the national flower of Costa Rica. It is a lovely and reliable late winter bloomer.

(those resulting from an exact crossing of *C. skinneri* with *C. aurantiaca*—or vice versa) will be quite uniform in color and shape, the color most often being a rose lavender or purple. However, we see colors varying from nearly cream-white, through yellow to shades of rose, onto orange and nearly to red, as a result of both inbreeding within populations of *C. Guatemalensis* as well as outcrossing either way to *C. skinneri* (lighter colors or more lavender) or to *C. aurantiaca* (oranges, roses, and reds). Indeed, this situation is so complex that many knowledgeable breeders feel that the best forms of *C. aurantiaca*—those with the more unusual coloration—are not straight *C. aurantiaca* at all, but rather the result of introgression with *C. skinneri*. This is not just speculation, either, as breeders have been able to duplicate observed natural results with artificially produced hybrids.

So far we've discussed quite a bit of orchidology, focusing on the genus *Cattleya*. As with so much pertaining to orchids, this genus is archetypal, and many of the same features that have been put forward thus far pertain to other members of its family group, the Laeliineae. Now we're going to move on to discuss some of the species in this group, still focusing on true *Cattleyas*, before moving on to the hybrids in this group, where we'll learn a little more about the "other" members of the Laelineae.

## The species

There are simply too many plants comprising *Cattleya* species to single out any more than a few. Most authorities agree that there are approximately 50 species in the genus *Cattleya*, and when its sister genera *Brassavola*, *Rhyncolaelia* (considered as *Brassavola* for hybrid registration purposes), *Sophronitis*, *Broughtonia*, *Epidendrum*, *Encyclia*, *Diacrium* or *Caulathron* (depending on how accurate you want to be), and *Barkeria*—the list goes on. Some are represented by a single species, some by several; a few have a broad variety of species well known and popular with hobbyists, others are for the specialist only. Many are available in cultivation as seed-grown or tissue-cultured plants, others as divisions.

The genus *Cattleya* has classically been, and appropriately still is, divided into two types: bifoliates and unifoliates. This division is straightforward—bifoliates have two or more leaves crowning their pseudoulbs, unifoliates (usually) only one. This artificial system is valuable to help us to categorize what otherwise might be a little unwieldy.

## Bifoliates

Bifoliates generally have relatively longer, more "cane-like" growths, with two or more (up to five in rare cases) leaves, smaller blooms often with a "spade" lip, and a more highly seasonal growth habit. Most grow at lower elevations and are less tolerant of low temperatures. Other generalizations may be made, but there would be more exceptions with these further generalizations. For example, there are usually more flowers to the inflorescence (flower head) in bifoliates—up to 30 or more in *C. guttata*—but there may only be one as in *C. walkeriana*. Colors tend to be

---

Overleaf: *C. intermedia* is a common bifoliate from Brazil, whose commercial growers have made remarkable strides in breeding improved forms.

Right: *B. nodosa* is popularly known as the "Lady of the Night" orchid for its beautiful nocturnal perfume.

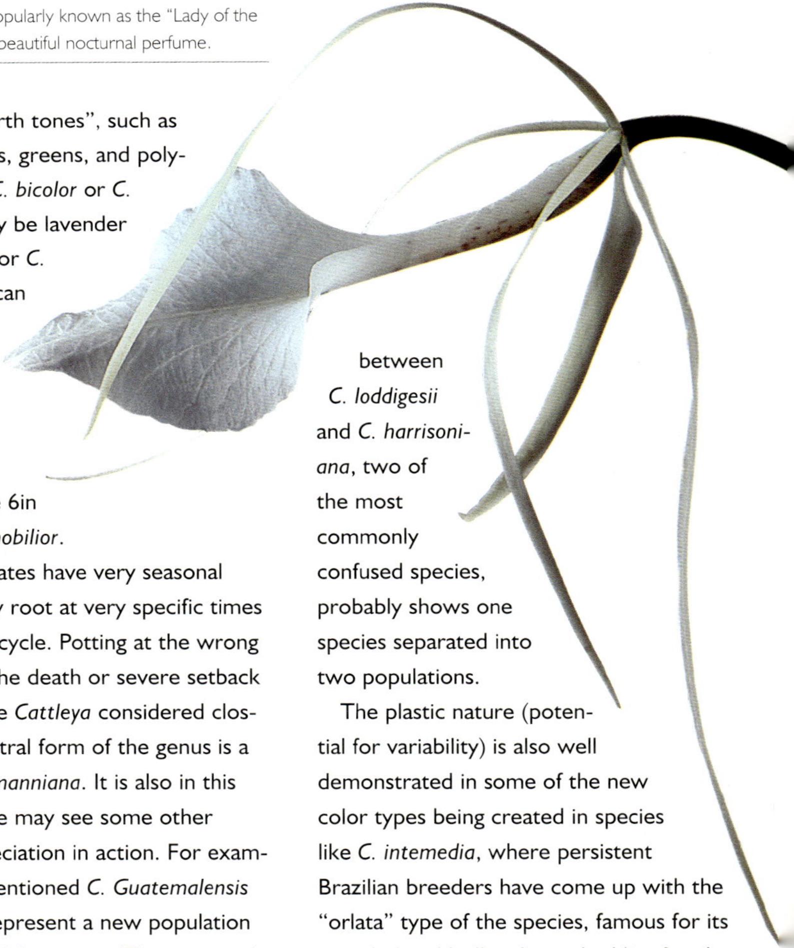

more in the "earth tones", such as bronzes, browns, greens, and polychromes, as in *C. bicolor* or *C. velutina*, but may be lavender as in *C. skinneri* or *C. violacea*. Plants can be quite tall, up to 5ft or more as in *C. leopoldii*, but may only be 6in or less as in *C. nobilior*.

Most all bifoliates have very seasonal growth and only root at very specific times in their growth cycle. Potting at the wrong time results in the death or severe setback of the plant. The *Cattleya* considered closest to the ancestral form of the genus is a bifoliate, *C. dormanniana*. It is also in this group where we may see some other examples of speciation in action. For example, the aforementioned *C. Guatemalensis* complex may represent a new population in the process of formation. The intergrade between *C. loddigesii* and *C. harrisoniana*, two of the most commonly confused species, probably shows one species separated into two populations.

The plastic nature (potential for variability) is also well demonstrated in some of the new color types being created in species like *C. intemedia*, where persistent Brazilian breeders have come up with the "orlata" type of the species, famous for its rounded and brilliantly marked lip. Another favorite in this group is the dwarf-growing Brazilian species, *C. walkeriana*. Perhaps no other *Cattleya* species has seen so much improvement, and has made such an impact on hybridizing recently. Its multiple good features include compact growth habit, long-lasting blooms, heavenly perfume, and ease of windowsill culture.

## Unfoliates

By contrast, unifoliates are much more uniform in their growth and flower habit. The growths are more obviously bulb-like with central thickening and with, of course, only one terminal leaf. (However, unifoliate hybrids may often have bifoliate growths, especially as younger plants.) Flowers are usually larger (to eight inches or more in species like *C. warscewiczii* and *C. mossiae*), fewer (two to five being typical), and, as a rule, lavender with darker markings in the lip to attract the pollinator.

Many of the unifoliates grow at slightly higher elevations, where nights are cooler and days do not become quite so warm. Indeed, some unifoliates—such as *C. mossiae*—do not flower as well, if at all, in areas where summer nights are too warm. It is, of course, in the unifoliates that hybridizing has reached its highest expression owing to their range of color types and popularity as cut flowers for corsages. One of the most important developments of the 1990s was the distribution from their countries of origin of select seed-grown populations of these species. As a result, we have seen a proliferation of fine examples of both the typical, as well as the more unusual color forms such as semi-alba, coerulea (blue) and alba (white). Unifoliates are generally more tolerant of potting season, though it is always a good rule of thumb to pot when rooting is expected. This is especially critical in species like *C. dowiana*, which will simply die if potted at the wrong season.

But we are discussing *Cattleyas* as a whole, here, and not just the genus. Unfortunately, it is next to impossible to illustrate all of the many horticulturally important species in this group, let alone the many that are less well known but equally deserving of a place in collections. No discussion of *Cattleya* types would be complete without mention of the "Ladies of the Night," the night fragrant *Brassavolas* and the rhyncolaelias. While these were formerly considered to be in the same genus, and are still considered as such for registration purposes by the UK's Royal Horticultural Society, differences in growth habit and flower form make them easy to tell apart.

### *Brassavola*

A recent informal poll showed that *Brassavola nodosa* is the orchid that most orchid growers would hate to be without. Its exotically shaped blooms, borne through the year over quill-like foliage, have an exquisite night fragrance that cannot be matched. The counterpart to *B. nodosa* is *Rhyncolaelia* (syn. *Brassavola*) *digbyana*. Its growth habit is much more robust and *Cattleya*-like, with its large green blooms and heavily bearded lip; it also has a beautiful night perfume. When you see brassavola in the background of a large-flowered *Cattleya* type, it is most likely from this species. On the other hand, if the flower is smaller and more spidery in appearance with the distinctive growth habit, *B. nodosa* is the likely culprit. This species has been gaining increasing favor recently as a parent for attractive potted plant type orchids.

### *Laelia*

There are simply too many good *Laelias* to mention more than a few. *Laelia*s are broken into several distinct groups, the Mexican or "true" *Laelia*s and the Brazilian types, some of which are much more like unifoliate *Cattleya*s, while another group, the *rupicolous Laelias*, are perhaps more closely allied to *Sophronitis*.

Best known of the genus must be Mexican *L. anceps*. This exceptionally widespread species comes in a variety of colors and forms. This plant is becoming an increasingly popular horticultural subject both as a species and as a parent. One of its most endearing traits is its wide range of temperature-tolerance. Not only will it withstand temperatures down to freezing, but also it can handle higher temperatures that might phase other cold-tolerant types.

Right: *C. schofeldiana* is another rather rare bifoliate that was even less common before being raised from seed in commercial nurseries.

Below: *L. harpophylla*

Several closely related species include *L. xanthina*, valued in early yellow breeding, and *L. tenebrosa*. Last of these species are the rupicolous types, which grow largely in rocky habitats and may be a little more difficult to grow than some other *Cattleya* types. There are two subgroups within this class, the taller and the shorter. The taller types, exemplified by *L. flava*, *L. cinnabarina*, and *L. harpophylla*, are easier to grow, and have brilliantly colored blooms in shades of red, yellow, and orange. These have been important in the breeding of cluster type hybrids that brighten winter with their heads of starry flowers. The shorter types are much more difficult to accommodate, as they originate in very specialized habitats. While such species as *L. harpophylla*, *L. flava*, *L. mantiqueirae*, and *L. briegeri*, have showy and colorful blooms, and have had some affect on hybridizing, the fact remains that they are beyond the range of the abilities of many novice growers.

Its Brazilian counterpart, both in range of colors and in importance to hybridizing, is *L. purpurata*. Entire orchid societies in Brazil (where this is the national flower), are devoted to the nearly 300 different named varieties of *L. purpurata*. As with *Rhyncolaelia digbyana*, if a *Laelia* is present in a standard *Cattleya* hybrid, chances are pretty good that it is this species, valued for its vigor, flower carriage, and boldly colored lip.

## Other cattelyas and relatives

No color is more sought-after in orchids than red. Two of the brightest red species in the *Cattleya* alliance are *Sophronitis coccinea* and *Broughtonia sanguinea*. Both come from opposing, but equally challenging, habitats, and this has a profound effect on their culture as well as on the culture of their progeny. *Soph. coccinea* comes from higher elevations in the Organ Mountains of Brazil, where it enjoys high light, tempered by cooler temperatures, and even moisture. These conditions are not always easy to duplicate in cultivation and are also demanded to an extent by the progeny.

*Bro. sanguinea*, on the other hand, comes from lower elevations in Jamaica, where it is subject to high temperatures and dry conditions. *Bro. sanguinea* also comes in a range of color from red to yellow to peach to white, all of which have been taken advantage of by wily breeders. As we range further afield from the genus *Cattleya*, so too do we range in color, form, and habitat. *Schomburgkias* and *Caulathron* (a.k.a. *Diacrium* for registration purposes) *bicornutum* can be treated together owing to the similarities in their

Above: *L. flava*

growth habits. These often-large growing plants have a special affinity for ants, which often inhabit their hollow bulbs, much to the detriment of anyone trying to collect the plants!

Right: *L. mantiqueirae*

### *Epidendrum*

As a group the *Epidendrums* could fill volumes. As discussed earlier, this was the generic name given to all epiphytes in the early days of plant classification. *Epidendrum* has remained, until very recently, a sort of catchall name for a broad variety of related, but disparate, species. (A similar situation will be seen in the Old World genus, *Dendrobium*.) Today, with the advent of molecular cytogenetics—the science of classification based on gene sequencing—we are gaining better insight into what is, and isn't, truly an "epi." The names, which have been given to former members of *Epidendrum*, are legion: *Encyclia*, *Anacheilium*, *Neolehmanniana*, *Nanodes*, *Barkeria*, *Psychilus*, *Oerstedella*, and most recently, *Prosthechea*, to name a few.

What we now think of as "epis" or true *Epidendrums* are reed-stem types with the lip fully attached to the column. *Epi. ibaguense*, *Epi. cinnabarinum* and their hybrids, as well as an increasing variety of other showy types such as *Epi. pseudepidendrum*, represent this group in modern collections. The "bulb epis," or encyclias, have pronounced pseudobulbs and lips only partially attached to the column. Popular species in this group include *Enc. cordigera* (a.k.a. *Epi. atropurpureum*), *Enc adenocaula*, and *Enc. phoenicia*. The well-known "cockleshell" epis (now reclassified as *Prosthechea*) are represented by old favorites like *Pro. cochleata* and *Pro. prismatocarpa*. The list could go on and on.

## The hybrids

It would be futile to list all of the many fine *Cattleya* alliance hybrids available today. Indeed, it is important to treat hybrids as groups, or as types, as all too often illustrated plants do not remain available in the trade, though similar (often better!) examples will be. For this reason, there is far more utility in informing about types, and about terminology, than about specific plants. There are a variety of factors to consider when thinking about *Cattleya* hybrids, including:

- Flower size
- Color type
- Season
- Plant size

Below: *L. briegeri*.

For example, a large fall purple might be *Blc.* "Amy Wakasugi." There are many similar hybrids available in this description, many of them often better. Another example might be the hybrids available from *Blc.* Oconee, or *Blc.* Bryce Canyon, or *Blc.* Mem. Crispin Rosales. Large winter whites are best exemplified by *C.* Bow Bells.

Bow Bells was the progenitor of a race of modern polyploid whites, of which there are simply too many to enumerate. Good semi-albas are not as common, but *Lc.* Mildred Rives or *Lc.* Starting Point, though older hybrids, retain their quality. *Blc.* Twentyfour Carat is a good example of a concolor yellow. Yellows often come with red lips and are sometimes known as semi yellow.

Cluster types are always popular and welcomed during dull winter months. *Slc.* Kauai Starbright and its related hybrids fit the bill here. Often, a small-growing hybrid is what is desired, the more so if it gives the promise of flowering throughout the year. Broughtonia hybrids, such as *Ctna.* Whynot, fill this niche. Blues such as *Lc.* Alarcon or *Lc.* Canhamiana are known as coeruleas and flower throughout the year with a peak in summer months. *B. nodosa* breeding is deservedly popular. *Bc.* Richard Mueller typifies this group. Spots, stripes, and more, are available in *Cattleya* hybrids. Only that of the breeders exceeds your imagination.

## The culture

*Cattleya*s were, for many years, the first orchid of aspiring hobbyists and were also the most widely grown of all orchids, primarily for cut flowers. This has changed in the last 20 years; *Cattleya* culture has remained the base point from which all other orchid culture is described. "Cooler than," "brighter than," "wetter than," "warmer than," *Cattleya*s—these specifications and more are frequently seen cultural descriptions for a broad range of orchids. Of course, not all *Cattleya*s grow alike, but the culture for standard, or cut-flower type, is a consistent and useful starting point.

In general, *Cattleya*s need strong, but not direct, light. This is best described as about 40%–60% of full sunlight or that available at an east or west, or lightly shaded south window. The plants will grow naturally firm and upright, needing no staking under proper light conditions, and their color will be a light olive green. Dark green, "floppy"

Above: *L. purpurata* "Rubra" is just one of the hundreds of color forms of this most popular of all Brazilian *Laelia* species. Closely related to *Cattleyas*, this species has been very important in the breeding of modern *Laelio cattleyas*.

plants are not getting enough light. Poor light quality is the number one reason why *Cattleyas* fail to flower. Smaller hybrids and species are preferable in the home, as it is easier to get good light to smaller plants than to larger. *Cattleyas* require a period of darkness to complete their metabolic processes. If they get overlong day length—perhaps accidentally by a reading lamp or street light, or intentionally to compensate for poor light quality—they will grow poorly and may not flower. Seasonal day length differential is important, too, to trigger flowering responses. *Cattleyas* need a fast-draining, open medium that holds some water but will also allow air circulation to the roots. The plants require a degree of drying between watering to allow the roots to breath. Overwatered plants exhibit the same symptoms as underwatered, because the roots will have died and are unable to take up any water. Temperatures should generally be moderate. That is, day temperatures should be around 80°F, though higher is permissible with increased humidity and air circulation, and lower may be inevitable owing to climatic conditions. Night temperatures should drop to a minimum of 15°F from the day temperatures, to ensure proper metabolic functioning; 60°–65°F is the normal recommendation, though the plants will tolerate both lower and higher if unavoidable.

Temperature, watering, and humidity, should be in balance. Higher temperatures, often accompanied by higher light, will demand more frequent watering and higher humidity. Conversely, lower temperatures will slow the plant's metabolism and subsequently, water needs, which should be attended by lower humidity. Ideally, humidity should be in the 50%–60% range, but should rise and fall with the temperature. Feeding should be appropriate to the medium in use and given "weekly, weakly." In other words, fertilize lightly and often, rather than infrequently and heavily. A good regime is to fertilize one half to one quarter strength (depending on season and your location) weekly.

A well-grown *Cattleya* will have upright, medium to light green foliage, and have an overall appearance of health. It will be firm in the pot, with green-tipped white roots. Flowering will be regular in the appropriate season. If you follow these guides you'll be proud of your accomplishment!

Above: *C. trianaei* growing in situ in its native Colombia. This species blooms in winter and is another very important link in the creation of our modern hybrid lines.

# CYMBIDIUM

Until very recently it could have been fairly stated that there were as many or more *Cymbidium* plants in cultivation than any other genus or type. *Cymbidiums*, or "cyms," were grown by the hundreds of thousands throughout the United States, Europe, New Zealand, and Australia, as well as in smaller numbers in other countries, as one of the staple cut-flower orchids. Breeders and growers contrived to extend the spring flowering season both earlier into the fall and later into June by cultural techniques and speculative breeding. Aided by growers in the opposing hemisphere, a thriving cut-flower industry has been able to provide *Cymbidium* blooms nearly year round. In common with cattleyas, the surplus plants spun off from the cut-flower growers fueled a rapidly growing potted plant industry, centered largely in southern and central California. Not only are cyms free-growing and reliable bloomers in such a Mediterranean climate, propagating freely by division and "back-bulbs," but they were the first orchids to be easily meristemmed on a large-scale basis, adding to their commercial appeal.

Yet only a relative few of the more than 40 known species have contributed in any meaningful way to the hybrid complex we know today. Nor are *Cymbidium* species particularly beloved of those who specialize in the growing of orchids. Yes, there are

Above: *Cym.* Christmas Beauty "St. Francis" is a classic pre-Christmas, or "early," cymbidium, long the mainstay of the cut-flower industry.

Right: *Cym.* Emotional Rescue "Everglades" are a fine example of modern warmth-tolerant cymbidiums. (HCC/AOS)

wonderful subjects for the species lover in this group, but, for some reason, the plants do not spark the same interest as do the species cattleyas, or paphs, or of so many other groups that have given rise to popular hybrid groups. The focus on hybrids in this genus—for there are essentially no worthwhile intergeneric hybrids involving *Cymbidium*—is uniquely Western, though, as species, cyms were among the first orchids to excite admiration among civilized peoples of the East. Indeed, both Chinese and Japanese cultures still prize certain *Cymbidium* species cultivars above all other orchids for their consistently graceful foliage, shyly beautiful blooms, and enchanting fragrance.

The history of cultivated orchids really started with *Cymbidiums*, as one of the very first mentions of orchids was by the Chinese philosopher Confucius in circa 500 BC. The many virtues of *Cym. ensifolium* were extolled and the name *lan* was given, signifying grace, dignity, and perfume. Indeed, *Cymbidiums* continue to be an

Left: *Cym.* Florida Flamingo "Pink Passion"—warmer-growing *Cymbidiums* are know for their showy lip patterns. (AM/AOS)

important part of Eastern culture to this day. The J. Matsnoka wrote perhaps the earliest known cultural information in 1725:

> In spring do not place out-of-doors.
> In summer do not expose to too much
> sun.
> In fall do not keep too dry.
> In winter do not keep too wet.

This remains good advice in many areas! Eastern sensibility in *Cymbidiums* remains distinctly different from the Occidental view. Graceful foliage and perfume are still highly prized over garish blooms. The most valuable plants are closely held and seldom propagated, as the scarcity is thought to enhance their value. Today, with the expansion of Asiatic culture across the world, we begin to see and to understand their joy in these dainty plants with their modest flowers. Even Japanese hybrid *Cymbidiums* have a distinct look and cultural needs.

In the West, and in England in particular, *Cymbidiums* were at first poorly understood and not highly prized. Even though the genus was one of the earliest to be established by Linnaeus (1799 on *Cym. aloifolium* and *Cym. ensifolium*), the plants known in cultivation were considered novelties at best and took up more space than many growers were willing to give them. Indeed, they were considered to be of so little interest that the pioneering hybridizer, John Dominy, didn't even bother to make any hybrids in the genus, leaving it to his successor, Seden, to make and flower the first *Cymbidium* hybrid, Vietchii (a.k.a. *Eburneo-lowianum, eburneum x lowianum*), in 1889. The only other hybrid of the 19th century was the nondescript *Cym. Winnianum* (*giganteum x mastersii*) of 1892. This was long after the first hybrids in other genera had begun to bloom and to be used for further breeding. Three other hybrids were registered in 1902, but the first hybrid, *Cym. Eburneolowianum*, combining as it did two of the three most important early parents, was the necessary prelude to what must be the single most important event in cym hybridizing, *Cym. Alexanderi*.

None of what we know today as *Cymbidiums* would be possible without *Eburneo-Lowianum* and, especially, *Cym. insigne*. This latter plant was discovered in

Left: *Cym. ultimatum*, "Santa Barbara"

Above: *Cym.* Sweet Dreams. "Everglades Mist"—sweet fragrance is another plus for the warmer growing *Cymbidiums*. (HCC/AOS)

the very early years of the 20th century in what is now Vietnam and provided the impetus for a new round of *Cymbidium* hybridizing and popularity. It is easy to see why *C. insigne* did so much for *Cymbidiums*; inflorescenses of lovely pink blooms standing straight and tall above the compact, gracefully arching foliage created the very image of what we today see as cymbidiums. With the showing of *Cym. Alexanderi* "Westonbirt" and its FCC/RHS in the early 1920s, modern *Cymbidiums* were born.

Even as their popularity declined with the end of the 20th century, *Cymbidiums* have remained a vital part of orchid history for two compelling reasons. First, the extraordinary dominance of parents like *Cym. Alexanderi* "Westonbirt," *Cym. Pauwelsii* "Comte d'Heptainne," and "Swallow" were never clearly understood, though recognized, until the pioneering research of Dr. Gustav Mehlquist uncovered the role of polyploidy. The three above-named plants were studied by Dr. Mehlquist in the late 1940s and discovered to be tetraploid. The normal genetic complement is known as diploid or 2n, and when this is doubled, to tetraploid or 4n, the resulting parent is more dominant in passing along its traits to its progeny. There are multitudes of ramifications that go with this knowledge, which is not unique to orchids, but it is enough to know here that this discovery led to the elucidation of polyploidy in other genera, notably cattleyas, as well as in many other *Cymbidiums*.

While tetraploidy was a chance mutation in the first individuals found, we have since learned how to artificially induce this condition, as well as breed for it by crossing known tetraploids together. We have, as a result, a race of modern hybrid *Cymbidiums* vastly finer than anything that could reasonably be expected from regular diploid hybridizing.

The second contribution of *Cymbidiums* to orchid history was their paving of the way for rapid and reliable cloning. Orchids, particularly very fine ones, do not come completely true from seed and the best may be as rare as one or fewer in a thousand. If the rare good one can only be reliably propagated by vegetative methods, the relatively slow process leads to high prices and slows breeding progress. Researchers searching for a way to free potatoes from virus chanced upon a technique that allowed rapid and exact propagation in vitro. It is unclear whether Morel of France or Wimber of the U.S. was the first to really apply the technique successfully, but it is certain that Morel was the first to publish his findings, though Wimber was not far behind.

Above: *Cym.* (Venetian Interlude x Globetrotter)—Intermediate *Cymbidiums*, with miniature species in their background, make excellent display subjects.

With the discovery of *in vitro* propagation

Above: *Cym.* "Sleeping Angel"—so-called "pure color" types lack anthocyanin (red) pigments and, as a result, are very long lasting.

in the early 1960s, and its proliferation throughout the industry by the early 1970s, exact replicas of fine hybrids became commonplace and available to nearly every interested grower. These same techniques, applied to other orchid genera as well as other plant types, have led to a revolution in both the potted plant and the cut-flower industries, where uniform high quality can now be assured. Production costs have continued to lower with new technology, enabling a rapid and vast growth in the availability of well priced and uniformly high

Right: *Cym.* Strathdon "Cooksbridge Noel" is one of the most satisfactory miniatures for pot culture owing to its compact stature and freedom of bloom. (AM/AOS)

*Cym.* Peachlet "Irene"

quality plants, both for the amateur and the professional.

## The species

Perhaps half of the approximately 44 recognized species are relatively commonly seen in cultivation. Few, if any, can make any great claim to popular appeal. This is not easy to understand, as a few, at least, are among the most beautiful of all orchids. Those that are not classically beautiful per se, are interesting at least and attractive at best. If a guess had to be made as to just why *Cymbidiums* species lacked public appeal, it would have to be that the plants are often large and can sometimes be considered coarse.

*Cymbidiums* species can also have more exacting temperature and light requirements than many other orchids, leading to the misapprehension that they are hard to grow or difficult to flower. Both of these illusions can be true to some extent, but neither is strictly true, and some species, at least, are more than worth the extra space and trouble. There are three main groups or types that concern us here; all are in cultivation to a greater or lesser degree, as well as having relevance in the hybrid picture.

## Warm-growing *Cymbidiums*

This type of *Cymbidium* has been in cultivation the longest and is common in Chinese horticultural history. It includes species such as *Cym. sinense*, *Cym. goeringii*, *Cym. ensifolium*, and *Cym. kanran*. All have arching graceful foliage that often forms the main attraction for the plant. They have also been in cultivation for so long that many horticultural varieties have been discovered and named, some of which are quite bizarre, beautiful only for their distinctiveness, while others are truly lovely with varying degrees of variegation or other foliar anomalies. Such varieties may be more difficult to grow or to grow well, and often fetch outrageous prices on the rare occasions when they reach the market.

*Cym. sinense*, *ensifolium*, and *kanran*, have straight spikes of several or more blooms, which may or may not emerge from the grassy, upright leaves; while *Cym. goeringii* has single flowers borne down in the more petite foliage. All three have been selected and propagated over the centuries for their foliar and floral abnormalities. Only *Cym. ensifolium* has played any significant role in further hybridizing, giving rise to a race of heat-tolerant and often quite early flowering varieties. The two most important parents to arise in this group are *Cym.* Peter Pan and *Cym.* Golden Elf, both of whose contributions will be discussed later.

### Tropical *Cymbidiums*

This group of *Cymbidium* species has earned a permanent place in cultivation and contains the species on which the genus *Cymbidium* was founded in 1799, *Cym. aloifolium*. Other species include *bicolor*, *dayanum*, *caniliculatum*, *chloranthum*, *madidum*, and *suave*. The range of this group extends from India through Indo-China and into Australia, where the bulk of the most popularly grown plants originate.

These orchids are characterized by stiff, leathery (coriaceous) foliage, and are very often epiphytic, requiring high light levels with abundant heat and humidity to flower. Only when their needs are met will the grower be rewarded with cascading

Right: *Cym.* Golden Elf "Sundust" is one of the most fragrant and heat-tolerant of all hybrid *Cymbidiums*, which has resulted in its becoming a popular potted flowering plant in the mass-market. (HCC/AOS)

inflorescenses of smallish blooms. Colors range from the apple green of *Cym. chloranthum* and some varieties of *Cym. madidum*, to the wine color of *Cym. canaliculatum*. Growers in tropical areas like south Florida have found that some species will naturalize well where they can be protected from the coldest weather, otherwise they must be grown in the highest available light conditions with the understanding that they may not flower every year. Owing to their size and finicky nature, species in this group have not been overly influential in hybridizing, although exceptions will follow in the next section.

### Cool summer *Cymbidiums*

The last, and arguably most important, collection of species are those originating in the middle elevations of the Himalayas, with one addition from Japan, *Cym. floribundum* (formerly *pumilum*). Here we find those plants that lay people recognize as

*Cymbidiums*, including such well-known species as *Cym. traceyanum*, *lowianum*, *insigne*, *sanderae*, *eburneum*, and *erythrostylum*. These are the showy species that have made the major contribution to the hybrid complex so beloved among orchid growers.

Modern hybridists have the advantage of years of selection to have the very best examples of these plants; both to produce select strains of the species, as well as improved hybrids. But it is the species with which we are most concerned here: the petite charm of *Cym. floribundum* flowering in the late fall and early winter; the exquisite perfume and exotic coloration of the fall-flowering *Cym. traceyanum*; the sparkling whiteness of the early season *Cym. erythrostylum*; *Cym. insigne*'s towering spikes of pink flowers in mid-spring contrasting with the single perfect white flowers of *Cym. eburneum* and, finally, *Cym. lowianum*'s profuse display of brilliant green blooms late in the spring. Such sights define *Cymbidiums*—indeed, orchids—for many dedicated growers in areas where these plants are appropriate garden subjects. Areas like coastal southern California, most of New Zealand, and much of coastal Australia, as well as South Africa, have a cadre of aficionados who will grow nothing else in their cool summer gardens.

Left: *Cym. erythrostylum*, a pre-Christmas blooming plant from Southeast Asia, has had a profound influence on the style and appearance of modern *Cymbidium* hybrids.

## The hybrids

Modern *Cymbidium* hybrids are a diverse and complex group that, despite being based on one genus (unlike other groups treated herein) and on a relatively few species, nearly defy categorization. Indeed, it is more productive to discuss the major types in a few short words, and go on to the exceptions!

The first hybrids to gain wide popular acceptance were those based in *Cym. Alexanderi* "Westonbirt" and other early chance tetraploids. Seven or eight of the large-flowered Himalayan species account for over 90% of all cym hybrids. These are, as a whole, pastel flowers of moderate size and good keeping quality with a main flowering season around March and April. In recent years, the range of colors and flowering period has expanded enormously. Notable improvements have been in early (before Christmas) season varieties and in high color types, where brilliant and unusual tones have become commonplace.

As *Cymbidiums* became more popular and available, breeders began to search for ways to make the plants more compact and satisfactory as potted subjects. The son of the famous H. G. Alexander made the pioneering hybrid in what was to become known as "miniature" *Cymbidiums* just before his death in World War 2. *Cym.* *Minuet*, *Cym. floribundum* or *pumilum* as it was then known, went on to produce an entirely new type of *Cymbidium*, including the aforementioned "miniatures"—those with *Cym. floribundum* as an immediate parent, and the "novelties"—those with *floribundum* in their ancestry. We could end our discussion of *Cymbidium* hybrids here, and have pretty much covered an enormously satisfying group of plants. However, we would be ignoring some of the most entertaining hybrids, as well as a group that is proving to be one that is greatly broadening the scope of those who can successfully grow and flower *Cymbidiums*.

It is in the warmth-tolerant hybrids, those that will bloom in warm-summer areas, where the most recent progress has been made. With the use of *Cym. ensifolium* and its two seminal hybrids, Peter Pan and Golden Elf, a race of fine new horticultural types has been born. Without the contribution of Mehlquist's research on polyploidy, and Wimber's pioneering work on its induction, we would not have these as parents, as they both breed poorly (and rarely) in their natural diploid forms. Breeders in Australia and New Zealand have led the way in the use of species like *Cym. madidum* and *caniliculatum*, as well as *Cym. devonianum*, to produce small-flowered hybrids with cascading inflorescenses so satifactory as hanging basket subjects.

## The care

Unfortunately, *Cymbidiums* make poor houseplants. In areas where they cannot be grown out-of-doors for a good part of the year, it is futile to even attempt to grow them. Where they can be given good quality bright light—in many cases full sunlight for a good portion of the day—and where summer nights are not too warm (over 60°F), reasonable success can be attained. Most growers need not concern themselves with the more specialized care needed by the less often seen and esoteric hybrids reserved for the cognoscenti, realizing that should they wish to grow and flower such hybrids, they will certainly require a greenhouse. Other hybrids, those most commonly seen, tend all to conform to the same general culture.

As already mentioned, bright light is the first key to successfully growing and flowering cyms. Their foliage should be a light medium green, naturally erect to slightly arching. Dark green, soft foliage is a sure indicator of poor quality light. A good, general rule is that the hotter the summer, the more mid-day shade the plants will enjoy, while cooler summer areas will allow the grower to give the plants nearly full sun. Most all commonly available cyms were bred from species that have a "hemi-epiphytic" habit. That is, they grow on the forest floor in the accumulated humus and duff, but not really in soil per se. Therefore, they will do best grown in a rich media that drains well but retains even moisture content. No *Cymbidium* likes to be allowed to go completely dry. Most plants, too, will be seasonal growers, requiring a high nitrogen content fertilizer during their period of growth, generally the spring and summer months, followed by a severe reduction or elimination of nitrogen in early fall to stimulate flowering.

While growers in areas such as southern California and the Antipodes can grow cyms year round as garden subjects, many others can succeed by growing the plants out-of-doors during frost-free months, and moving them indoors to a sunroom or cool porch during the winter months. However, unless late summer and early fall night temperatures drop into the low 60s°F and high 50s°F, many hybrids—particularly those that flower before Christmas—simply will not bloom. The exceptions are those that have been bred for warmth-tolerance from such parents as Peter Pan, Golden Elf, and a few other related hybrids, which flower in areas like the Gulf Coast states and south Florida.

# DENDROBIUM

Above: *Den. capilipes* gives a beautiful display in winter months.

Right: *Den. bullenianum* (*syn. topazicum*) is a member of the Pedilonum section and flowers off second-year canes.

Quite simply, this is a genus of superlatives. No other genus will be so difficult to encapsulate in the allotted space. Comparisons with other genera can be made, but such comparisons are seldom exclusive or completely apt. One such comparison might be with *Cymbidium*, where intergeneric hybrids are essentially absent; or with the closely allied and equally diverse genus *Bulbophyllum*, whose plant and flower dimensions, as well as habitat range, are nearly as broad in scope as those of *Dendrobium*. However, few, if any, genera have the sheer geographical sweep of *Dendrobiums*.

This Old World genus covers areas from India, across southeast Asia into Australia in the south, and Japan and Taiwan in the north. Remarkably, elevations from sea level to over 10,000ft. will harbor *Dendrobiums*, as will near deserts, seasonally dry forests, and some of the wettest

areas on earth. *Dendrobiums* are, by and large, epiphytes, with only a relative few finding lithophytic or quasi-terrestrial modes favorable. Flowers can be measured in fractions of an inch or over four inches; ephemeral, lasting only hours, or among the longest-lasting of all blooms to over six months or more; dingy brown to brightest scarlet, or yellow, or orange, and on to purest sparkling white.

*Dendrobium* plants themselves may be less than a quarter of an inch tall, or over ten feet. Many species inhabit seasonally dry, often monsoonal climates, and so are deciduous; while other species will retain their leaves for a period of years. And even though the species are found in so many different climes at such a variety of elevations, few are tolerant of frost and so may generally be thought of as tropical plants. Even in this instance, though, species from the extremes of the genus' range in Japan or in Australia may occasionally be subject to temperatures below freezing. In an ironic twist, many species rely on seasonal temperature contrasts to initiate flowering. Such changes may be brought on by a cold and dry season, or by temperature drops caused by the heavy cloud cover and rains of a monsoon.

It is the sheer size and diversity of the genus that render it so difficult to treat effectively. Both classical and modern authors are unanimous in their assessment of this group as "confusing." Like other large genera such as *Epidendrum*, *Bulbophyllum*, and *Pleurothallis*, *Dendrobium* may prove to be an artificial assemblage: that is, a group of plants with superficial similarities not borne out by close genetic relationships. Chromosome mapping and the resultant cladistic analysis being carried out today on the frontiers of taxonomic research will certainly result in a change in the way we now look at the genus. With many more than 1,200 validly described species, taxonomists over the years have attempted to separate out different genera from the concept of *Dendrobium*—the type species of which is the Japanese native, *Den. moniliforme*—with varying degrees of success. There are fairly clear-cut groups into which the varying members of the

Left: *Den.* "Gatton Sunray" qualifies as a "survivor" having been bred in the later part of the 19th century and remaining common today. (FCC/RHS)

Above: *Den.* Autumn Carnival "Impact" is a wonderful example of the heights reached by modern Phalaenanthe breeding. (AM/AOS)

genus fall, as evidenced by floral and foliar characters, as well as by breeding characteristics, i.e. ease of production and fertility of offspring. In other words, the various groups of *Dendrobium*s are defined as much by the fact that they will breed among themselves, producing fertile progeny, as that they will often not breed between disparate groups.

For these, and other reasons, this chapter will depart from the format of other chapters—overall discussion, species, hybrids, care—and treat each group in turn. In each group, we will discuss the species and the hybrids, as well as the care unique to the particular type. Some groups will be represented mainly by species, others almost exclusively by hybrids. Some groups will be easy for the average grower; others beyond the reach of all but the most sophisticated. It is especially important to know your conditions and climatic limitations when it comes to succeeding with *Dendrobiums*. There will always be a plant or plants that are perfect for the conditions you are able to provide, in the same way there will be plants with which success will be elusive, if attainable at all, in your area. On top of this, the various groups, also known as sections, within *Dendrobium* don't always have popular names, so you will have to learn the Latin terms. This will help you, though, with knowing more precisely what type of plant you have so that you can better know how to care for it.

## THE SECTIONS

### Phalaenanthe

Popularly known as the "*Phalaenopsis* type" or "den phals" after their flowers' resemblance to the moth-like blooms of the genus *Phalaenopsis*, these are one of the world's most widely grown orchids. If you've been given a flowering *Dendrobium* plant as a gift, chances are pretty good that it is one of these. Because this type is so widely grown, the plants may not be labeled beyond simply "*Dendrobium* orchid." You'll recognize them by their cane-like growth with leaves held at about 90° and arching inflorescenses emerging near the top of the pseudobulbs, carrying eight to 12 or more blooms. While the most commonly seen colors are lavenders and whites, more exotically colored and striped clones are coming into cultivation at a rapid pace.

The species in this section originate in Indonesia, New Guinea, and Australia and are considered among the easiest to grow of the genus. Commonly seen are *affine*, *bigibbum*, *dicuphum*, *phalaenopsis* and *superbiens* as well as various combinations. The native habitats of the species in this group tend to have a lengthy, warm, moist growing season, followed by a slightly cooler dry season in late fall and winter months. This seasonal fluctuation affects their cultural needs. As with other members of the genus that grow in areas with distinct seasons, "den phals" require copious

watering and fertilizing during active growth, followed by a drier period with little, if any, nitrogen which would hinder flowering. The grower will recognize the onset of a resting period with the maturation of the pseudobulb, shown by the production of a terminal leaf. This most often occurs in late summer into fall, and unless nitrogen is reduced or eliminated during this season, flowering may be retarded or prevented. The plants will appreciate strong light, year round, much like that for cattleyas, and prefer warm growing conditions along with the light, to make up strong growths.

One of the most common mistakes growers make with this section, and a problem common with other types of *Dendrobium*, is overpotting. The plants will grow far better, with a stronger root system, if kept in proportionately small pots. The closely coupled growths do not mind being at the edge of the pot, and the more rapid drying will allow the frequent watering and fertilizing that will give the best growth. The best advice is to pot for the bottom (the roots) and not for the top.

Left: *Den. lindleyei* (*syn. aggregatum*) is a popular member of the Callista section and flowers profusely in late winter after a dry season.

## Spatulata

Also known as "antelope" types, for their distinctive flower form, this is another of the most widely cultivated groups of *Dendrobium*. The often-large plants are native to lower elevations in the islands of the South Pacific, as well as tropical Australia, where they experience hot and humid growing conditions. Because of this, "antelope" species and hybrids are among the most sensitive to cold temperatures, and may experience leaf-drop even as a result of a cold draft. The plant habit is not dissimilar to the "den phal" types, and indeed, this is one of the few instances where intersectional hybrids are relatively common.

*Den. canaliculatum* is the species most often used in this breeding line to give a profusion of floriferous spikes on compact plants. Other commonly seen species include *antennatum*, *stratiotes*, *strebloceras*, *discolor*, and *johannis*. The often-multiple inflorescenses are produced from the upper nodes of the tapering pseudobulbs, which can flower for several years in succession. This habit of multiple flowering from older canes coupled with

Right: *Den. bracteosum* gives a lovely display on deciduous canes.

Above: *Den. crumenatum*, one of the most ephemeral of all orchid flowers, lasts only a few hours and so relies on strong perfume to attract its pollinators from a distance.

heat-induced rapidity of growth, enables these plants to make superb specimens in areas with the appropriate climate.

Owing to their need for warm temperatures, very bright light—as much as for *Vandas*—and often prodigious size, plants in this group do best in more tropical areas, where they can be grown out-of-doors for at least part of the year. Temperatures below 60°F should be avoided, as leaf drop may occur. Plants do not experience any significant rest period in nature, though watering frequency may be reduced along with fertilizer as growths mature. While the species are showy indeed, hybrids are most commonly seen, as breeders attempt to retain the floriferous quality of the species parents, while reducing plant size.

## Latouria

This group has only recently seen a surge in popularity owing to Hawaiian influences. For this reason, it has no truly "popular" name, though they are often referred to as simply "New Guinea" types. Obviously, then, the species are found in New Guinea as well as the nearby Solomon Islands, where they grow in lower to middle elevations in warm and humid conditions with high light. Species such as *atroviolaceum*, *polysema*, *forbesii*, *macrophyllum*, and, especially, *spectabile*, are most commonly seen, while primary hybrids are becoming more frequently available.

*Den. spectabile* is one of this section's most popularly grown species, and is one of the orchid world's most bizarrely beautiful members. The very long-lasting blooms are borne on imposing plants, making for a decorative subject par excellence. Mature plants are beginning to appear at orchid shows and always excite comment. In general, flower colors are not bright in this group, favoring greens and ochres, with often near-black colors in the lips. Characteristics include hairy sepals and upright infloresenses.

Growing conditions are as for the *Spatulata* types, with a preference for slightly more drying between waterings. However, it would be accurate to say that the needs of these plants under artificial cultivation have not been completely worked out, and many growers find them to be extremely difficult to keep and very unreliable to bloom. So, these may be best left to more specialized growers for the foreseeable future, though those who succeed with them will find them worth the extra effort.

Above: *Den. hercoglossum*

## Dendrobium

This section includes both the well-known "Nobile" types as well as the type species for the genus, *Den. moniliforme*, as well as some of the best loved of all species. The plants generally consist of gently-drooping deciduous canes, with leaves all along their length, and one to several flowers at each node along the cane on well-flowered specimens. Flowers almost always appear

Above: *Den. nobile* is the species parent of so many popular hybrids that they are popularly knows as nobile-types.

during the times of year when the plants have dropped their leaves, and therefore give a lovely presentation.

The popularity of the "Nobile" *Dendrobiums* is largely due to the work of one man, Jiro Yamamoto of Japan, who developed *Den. nobile* and several closely related species into a major horticultural type. The rounded, *Cattleya*-like blooms appear up and down fat canes that resemble cigars. Colors run the gamut from white through lavender to yellows and pastels. While this type is frequently seen for sale during the spring months, it can be induced to flower at almost any season by manipulation of temperature and fertilizer. Not every grower manages to do well with "Nobiles," many finding that instead of flowers, they have plantlets, known as "keikis" (Hawaiian for baby) growing from the nodes. This results from the misapplication of nitrogen after the maturation of the cane(s). Successful growers give "Nobiles" all the light the plants can stand, lots of fertilizer and water while in active growth, cutting out nitrogen as canes approach maturity after mid-summer.

Growing season temperatures should be as for cattleyas. If plants are kept cool and on the dry side during this period, the canes will drop their leaves and reward with a profusion of blooms, one or a few at each node up and down the stem. The habit of producing keikis can be annoying, but older flowered canes will produce the offsets from unflowered nodes, and the plantlets can simply be popped off and potted up when roots show. First flowering will be in a year or two. The Japanese native *Den. moniliforme* has been introduced into this line of breeding to produce a race of hybrids that are smaller in size, as well as generally easier to flower and more tolerant of warmer conditions.

## Other species

Also in this section is a series of species including *anosmum* (formerly known as *superbum*), *aphyllum* (*pierardii*), *crassinode*, *fimbriatum*, *loddigesii*, *parishii*, and *primulinum*. All of these plants have more strongly pendant growth habit than the "Nobiles" and often do very well mounted on cork or treefern, where their need for seasonal dryness can be more easily accommodated. The raspberry-scented *Den. anosmum* is the beloved "Hono Hono" of Hawaii, where it is widely propagated and naturalized in trees. Similarly, *aphyllum* (much more often seen as *pierardii*) is

Right: *Den.* Christmas Chime "Asuka" is a superb example of a modern nobile type *Dendrobium*. (AM/AOS)

Below: *Den. findleyanum* is closely allied to *Den. nobile*, both being in the *Dendrobium* section of the genus.

widespread through gardens in the dry winter tropics and sub-tropics. When properly grown, members of this group will drop their leaves in late fall, and flowers will appear along the canes in late winter into early spring, giving a short-lived, but spectacular display. Elimination of excess nitrogen as the growing season draws to a close is critical in this group of species if flowers, rather than keikis, are the desired results. The plants will need little, if any, water while leafless.

### Dendrocoryne

Beloved of Australians, these "hard cane" species and hybrids are native to their land, and they have made the best of them. It is fitting to discuss these right after *Dendrobium*, because, like the "Nobiles," these won't bloom if over-fertilized or if not allowed a cool resting period.

Epitomized by *Den. kingianum*, this group also includes *gracilicaule*, *speciosum*, and *tetragonum*, among others.

Several achievements in this group are worthy of note. First and foremost, almost incredible advances have been made in the line breeding of superior strains of *kingianum*. Darker and rounder, or in a variety of colors ranging from the typical rose lavender, through to white, and white with a red lip, Australian breeders have made great progress with the basic species and have created a race of hybrids that fills the early spring months with brightly colored blooms, which are often sweetly perfumed. One of the most popular Australian natives is *Den. speciosum*, the "Rock Lily," which is sufficiently widespread to come in several distinct varieties. A plant cultivated from seed was recently awarded in Santa Barbara, California, where it had reached the size of a small car, growing out-of-doors alongside *Cymbidiums* and other cool orchids. The plant was covered by literally hundreds of inflorescenses bearing well over 10,000 flowers.

If these orchids have a drawback, it is that the flowers are relatively short-lived,

Above: *Den. aphyllum* (*syn. pierardii*) is another popular member of this group that drops its leaves prior to flowering in early spring.

lasting only two to three weeks. However, proper care can result in rewards like the above-mentioned *Den. speciosum*, and Antipodean spring orchid shows are often filled with large and floriferous examples of this type. The best growers provide *Cymbidium*-like conditions of cool to intermediate temperatures, very high light, regular fertilization during the growing

Right: *Den. secundum album* has inflorescences of white blooms.

season, while drying and cooling after maturation of growth for flower production. If a cool and dry rest is not given, the plants will produce keikis rather than flowers.

### Formosae

Formerly, and more familiarly, known as the "Nigrohirsutae" or black-hair group, for the fine black hairs that cover the canes. Originating in the Himalayas and southern China, into Borneo, the Philippines, and Malaysia, species in this group grow at a variety of elevations from the hot and humid lowland mangrove swamps through monsoon scrub and up to mountain cloud forests. Because they come from such a range of elevation, it is important to know the habitat of the species or parents of the hybrid in order to know how best to grow the particular plant. Cane size ranges from the miniature *bellatulum* up to the intermediate-sized *formosum* and *infundibulum*.

Other well-known species in this section are *cruentum*, *dearei*, *draconis*, *sanderae* and *trigonopsis*. Most have very long-lasting white blooms offset by a highly colored lip. Breeders formerly worked mostly with the taller species such as *formosum*, *sanderae*, and *infundibulum* to produce a race of hybrids with showy and large white blooms of exceptional keeping quality. In more recent years, Hawaiian breeders have been adding in *cruentum* and *bellatulum* to reduce plant size and increase the plant growability. This has also had the happy result of increasing flower count along the canes, as well as the season and frequency of bloom, which formerly was strictly limited.

Plants do best with the same, or slightly higher, light levels as cattleyas. Temperature preferences will depend a great deal on the constituent parents of the particular plant, but most will grow happily with cattleyas, that is, around 60°F at night and 80–85°F during the day. Underpot in well-drained medium as for most others in the genus, and keep evenly moist year round, with a slight drying rest as growths mature. As with almost all *Dendrobiums*, overfertilizing results in curtailed blooming. Well-grown plants may remain in bloom for months, making this group one of the best values for the space.

## Callista

If the best-known and most popular member of this section was still named *Den. aggregatum*, rather than *Den. lindleyi*, we would call this the "Aggregatum" group as this is by far the best-known and most popular member of the group. Other members of this widely grown group are *jenkinsii*, *chrysotoxum*, *densiflorum*, *farmeri*, and *thyrsiflorum*. These range from the middle elevations of the Himalayas east to Burma, Thailand, on into Laos and Vietnam and southwestern China. Most have prominent pseudobulbs and pendant infloresences,

Above: *Den. cuthbertsonii* is a new member of the high-altitude *Oxyglossum* centered in New Guinea.

Above: *Den.* Jester "Vicky Joy" is a hybrid in the difficult-to-photograph *Spatulata* section. (AM/AOS)

Above: *Den.* Yellow Stars "von S." is a hybrid in the Latouria group. (HCC/AOS)

often of brilliant yellow blooms. Very little hybridization has been done with these plants, perhaps because they are so beautiful on their own, or because the flowers are not especially long-lasting.

An interesting conservation note with these and several other Indian and Thai species, is that fewer are seen today than formerly, as the trade in wild-collected plants has become more difficult, if not impossible, and the demand is not enough to justify artificial propagation. This is a shame, not only for what it says about the conservation orientation of the industry, but because there are few more beautiful sights than a member of this section—*lindleyi*, *chrysotoxum*, or whatever—well bloomed in their spring season.

These plants' ease of culture is amply demonstrated by the facility with which growers can rather quickly raise a specimen plant. All it takes is high light, as for cattleyas, plenty of fertilizer and water during the growing period, followed by a pronounced rest after the growths mature. Indeed, conventional wisdom regards any water at all during the winter months as a sure preventative of flowering. For this reason, and because of the plants' general love of good air circulation around the roots, as well as their pendant flowering habit, these make excellent subjects for basket or slab culture. Only the smaller-growing *lindleyi* and *jenkinsii* are potential houseplants, and even then, they are marginal owing to their high light requirements.

## Oxyglossum

This and the next section are relative newcomers to popular cultivation, and are not too commonly seen outside of specialist circles. Nor has sufficient hybridizing been done in either group to establish any trends or lines with widespread public approval. Oxyglossum species are generally denizens of high-altitude cloud forests, where they enjoy overall cool conditions coupled with uniformly high humidity and constant moisture at the roots. Most are from New Guinea and almost all show a typical bird-pollination syndrome of red, orange and related hued flowers that are extraordinarily long lasting, often for months.

Perhaps most familiarly seen today is *Den. cuthbertsonii*, formerly known as *Den. sophronitis*, which has been raised from select sibling crosses in a wide variety of colors ranging from the typical red through candy-corn. Because the flowers are so long lasting, and because the plants grow so profusely under the right climatic regime, specimen plants of great beauty are shown each year, primarily in the Pacific Northwest. Other members of this group include *coerulescens*, *uncatum*, and *violaceum*. Proper cultural conditions are not

Right: *Den. miyakei* is a profuse bloomer that is easy to grow.

easily duplicated in cultivation, except where naturally occurring, so these can be among the most difficult of the genus for hobbyists to grow well. Bright, diffuse light should be coupled with cool temperatures and high humidity. The best plants seem to be grown in high quality sphagnum moss.

## Pedilonum

Another New Guinean section characterized by bird-pollination, with clusters of tubular, brightly colored flowers, members of this group can also be found in Malaysia, Thailand, and Indonesia. While some grow at higher elevations, these are generally mid-elevation plants.

Above: *Den. arachnites*, a member of the Callista group, is often confused with *Den. unicum*.

Conditions similar to those given the *Formosae* section will suit best, especially if accompanied by a brief fall rest period with bright light.

Canes generally take two years to mature and drop their leaves prior to flowering from top nodes. Cool to intermediate conditions are called for, in conjunction with the underpotting so typical of this genus. While still relatively obscure and specialist plants, such members of the group as *amethystoglossa*, *victoria-reginae*, *secundum*, *miyakei*, *topazicum* and *smiliae* are becoming more widely propagated. The real potential of the members of this section is still under evaluation, as seed raised plants continue to mature and demonstrate what they can do. It appears that some will enter mainstream horticulture owing to their multiple decorative features.

## A few more species

With a genus as large and diverse as this, a few "favorites" are bound to slip through the cracks and not get a mention. This is to be regretted. However, there is an—artificial, to be sure—group of *Dendrobiums* that never fail to excite interest for their foliage or growth habit alone. *Den. anceps*, *linguiforme*, *teretifolium* and *cucumerianum* are just plain fascinating as plants, with flowers that pale against the foliar interest. *Den. anceps* can be best compared to a vigorous *Lockhartia* or *Diachea*, with neatly braided leaves completely obscuring the thin canes. This is an excellent basket subject, where the cascades of braided leaves are sure to excite comment. *Den. teretifolium* has a pendant growth habit, showcasing the terete (pencil-shaped) leaves that give it its name. Both *linguiforme* and *cucumerianum* have a scrambling, rambling habit with growths closely appressed to the surface of the medium. *Den. linguiforme* has tongue-shaped leaves, while *cucumerianum*'s leaves look like gherkins! A mount of either of these species, well grown, is something to be proud of. The flowers of these last three species are remarkably similar and exceptionally spidery and nondescript, though a cloud of such blooms hovering over the odd plant can be quite sensational.

Above: *Den.* anceps is an orchid often grown for its overall fine appearance, as the flowers are relatively insignificant and usually hidden in the foliage.

# ONCIDIUM

Perhaps no other group of orchids is so beloved, yet so diverse. The Oncidiinae truly defy any overall statements. Taxonomists have striven over the years to determine alliances and relationships within this tribe, only to have other scientists immediately dispute their findings, or point out the obvious shortcomings of their determination. For example, the chief taxonomic separation between *Oncidiums* and *Odontoglossums*—the two best known and widely grown genera—is the angle between the column and the lip! Hardly something of vast evolutionary significance. Indeed, there is no "generic" name for the Oncidiinae, as there is for cattleyas or for pleurothallids, although many simply use "*Oncidiums*" to refer to the warmer growing types and "odonts" to refer to the cooler growers.

As with other large, aggregates such as dendrobiums and bulbophyllums, their habitat ranges from equatorial sea level to subtropical mountains at elevations more than 10,000ft. Flower size ranges from miniscule to more than 16in, plant size from the tiniest fan-shaped (equitant) types to rambling cloud forest denizens that can

Above: *Comparettia coccinea*

Above Right: *Onc. ampliatum* is often known as the tortoise-shell orchid for its unusual pseudobulbs.

reach lengths of a number of feet to the bulky "mule ears" with their single thick, heavy leaves. The common names conferred on members of this group tell a story of popularity. From the spider orchid (*Brassia*) to the lavender and old lace orchid (*Onc. ornithorhyncum*) to dancing lady orchid (*Onc. varicosum*) to the butterfly orchid (*Onc.* or *Psychopsis papilio*) beloved of the Duke of Devonshire, the diversity of color, form, scent, size, and degree of difficulty make this group of plants a perennial favorite with growers around the world.

*Onc. altissimum* and *Onc. carthagenense* were among the first orchids in the Kew collection, and appeared on an inventory taken in 1794. Both remain notable as easy orchids to grow. This makes their survival in the terrible conditions that must have been available in the stove-houses of the day more understandable. The Caribbean plant *Onc. variegatum* is the species on which the genus *Oncidium* was established in 1800. Ironically, and indicative of the taxonomic problems inherent there, *Onc. variegatum* is not typical of most plants in the genus. Today, most taxonomists believe that it should be placed in another genus entirely. Scientists and growers agree that *Onc. variegatum* should be in the genus *Tolumnia* along with other "equitant" or fan-shaped types that inhabit drier areas of the Caribbean as twig epiphytes.

Above: *Onc. sphacelatum* is one of the popular "Golden Shower" type ***Oncidiums***.

*Brassia* was established in 1813 and *Odontoglossum* in 1815, with *Odm. epidendroides* as the type species. While *Odm. epidendroides* is typical of many "odonts" it is definitely not what one thinks of when visualizing the group. Walking through a timeline of the *Oncidiinae* brings to light another important facet of early botany. While the genus *Odontoglossum* was first described as early 1815, the first living plant of an *Odontoglossum* did not reach Europe until 1835, when *Odm.* (now *Lemboglossum*) *bictoniense* made it to England alive. Again, we see how the changes in nomenclature can affect history, with the first odont to reach England no longer considered an odont! It was not until later in the century, when more living plants began to reach Europe safely, that descriptions were based on other than dried, pressed herbarium materials.

As the scope of exploration became greater, and as growing methods were better understood, more and more new plants found a home in collections. The Brazilian

*Miltonia spectabilis* entered England in the late 1830s, followed by the brilliant red *Cochlioda noezliana* in the mid-1850s. Many of the most beautiful members of this group came from higher elevations, and so were not well-adapted either for the voyage to Europe or to the wretched hot conditions they would find in the greenhouses of the time. It was Paxton's cultural breakthrough that enabled growers to keep a higher percentage of imported plants alive for longer.

Perhaps the showiest member of this group is *Odm. crispum*, an absolutely beautiful white bloom borne on an arching inflorescence of eight or more flowers, with 20 or more not uncommon. *Crispum*, along with *Coch. noezliana*, forms the backbone of our modern cool-growing odont complex. *Odm. crispum* comes from higher elevations in the Andes of Colombia. Literally hundreds of thousands of plants were imported into Europe and England in the late 1800s. For example, the well-known auction firm of Protheroe and Morris in 1889 advertised an auction lot of 10,000 plants of *Odm. crispum*, at what experts consider to be the peak of this orchid's

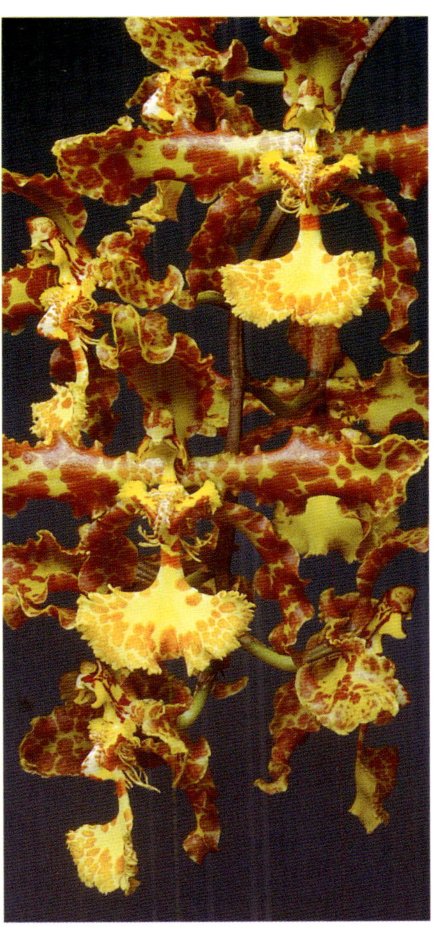

Above: *Onc. wittii* (long known as *Onc. stacyi*) is one of the showiest of the "rat tail" ***Oncidiums***.

popularity. Without the newly gained knowledge of the importance of fresh, moving air to the greenhouse, even fewer of these beautiful plants would have survived.

Orchid hybridization was becoming a well-known phenomenon by this time. Many presumptive natural hybrids in the *Odontoglossum* group came to light, and many growers believed that major floral variations were the result of such natural hybridization. Unfortunately, the techniques for raising odonts from seed lagged behind that of other genera.

Finally, and rather suddenly, late in the 19th century, growers were successful raising seedlings, which enabled breeders to confirm many of the putative natural hybrids. One of the most important hybrids has proven to be *Odm. Ardentissimum* (*crispum x pescatorei*), registered in 1898, which has given us both fine shape and large branching spikes.

A vast array of intergeneric hybrids soon followed, forming the basis for the current range in this group. Red odonts came with the first *Odontioda* (*Odontoglossum x Cochlioda*) in 1904, larger lips with *Odontonia* (*Odontoglossum x Miltonia*) in 1905, big sprays of flowers and warmth-tolerance with *Odontocidium* (*Odontoglossum x Oncidium*) in 1911, and, finally, the best of all worlds with the trigeneric *Vuylstekeara* (*Odontoglossum x Cochlioda x Miltonia*) also in 1911. While many of these original parents have been lost owing to the ensuing two World Wars, several still exist and are eagerly sought by odont fanciers. *Oda. Heatonensis* (*Coch. sanguinea x Odm. cirrhosum*), registered in 1906, remains in demand and in use as a parent.

Yet, as lovely as the odont group can be, standard *Odontoglossums* and odontiodas remain frustratingly difficult to grow in all but the coolest of climates. For this reason, much modern breeding focuses on the attempt to infuse warmth-tolerance into the breeding line with the use of *Oncidiums*, *Brassia* and other genera. However, it is important to stress that the beautiful odonts are just the tip of the iceberg in the Oncidiinae. There are so many worthwhile orchids to grow and enjoy in such a variety

Left: *Milt. spectabilis* Moreliana is the purple form of this popular and easy-to-grow Brazilian species.

Above: *Milt. spectabilis*, the typical form, is less commonly seen than Moreliana, whose color is more exciting to orchid growers.

of shapes, sizes and colors; and that grow in such a broad range of conditions that we can only "open the door a crack."

There is a natural division between both species and hybrids—those that need warmth or cool conditions to grow. The warmer growing plants are generally grown quite well under *Cattleya* conditions if given appropriate amounts of shade; with some requiring more light, some less. The cool-growing, higher elevation plants must be given abundant fresh air and temperatures that rarely exceed 75°F, with nights in the low 60s°F to high 50s°F. These types do very well in the Pacific Northwest, the Northeast, and in England. In addition, the cooler growing the plant, the more important good quality water, low in dissolved solids, will be.

## The species

There are simply too many worthwhile candidates to discuss more than a few from each group. We have already made a beginning on the cooler-growing types, with *Odontoglossum crispum* and *pescatorei* (now more properly known as *nobile*), as well as *Cochlioda noezliana*. *Miltonia vexillaria* and *roezlii* (both now better known as *Miltoniopsis*, as distinct from the warmer-growing true miltonias from Brazil) are also mid-elevation dwellers. These two species, along with the related *Milt. phalaenopsis*, have given rise to a very important group of hybrids, known as the "Pansy Orchids," which aptly describes their often beautifully patterned, lip-dominated blooms. Colombian *Miltoniopsis* are not strictly cool-growing, but resent wide temperature variation, and so are generally best grown in coastally moderated areas where nights are not too cold and days not too warm.

No discussion of higher-elevation, cooler Oncidiinae would be complete without mention of the *cyrtochilums*. While exact taxonomic status is still a bit up in the air, these cloud-forest dwellers can be among the showiest of the entire group. Most have a rambling, vine-like growth habit with a good distance—up to a foot or more

Right: *Odcdm.* Haytor "Black Gold" is a fine example of a warmer-growing ***Oncidium*** hybrid. (AM/AOS)

Above: *Onc. phalaenopsis*, closely related to *Onc. nubigenum*, is not one of the easiest species to grow.

in cases—between pseudobulbs. The inflorescences twine off through the vegetation, producing the often-showy blooms on side branches. The flowers are usually in shades of rich rust, mahogany, and gold. Along with *Odm. crispum* types, these require quite cool temperatures and good quality water to do their best.

It is easy to be sidetracked by the cool growers in the Oncidiinae. They are lovely and present a challenge that many orchidists just cannot resist. However, it is a mistake to ignore the many, many fine species that are available in this group that will grow happily under cattleya conditions or on a sunny windowsill in your home. Some, of course, are simply too large and requiring of high light to be good for anywhere but the greenhouse. The "golden shower" types exemplified by *Onc. sphacelatum* and *Onc. ampliatum* (the tortoise shell orchid for its unusually furrowed pseudobulbs) are wonderful in the greenhouse or, in warmer areas, on the patio. There are smaller growing cousins of these plants that will grow easily in home conditions. Among these is *Onc. onustum* and the range of Caribbean tolumnias, or equitant *Oncidiums*.

We must not forget, either, the orchids that really started it all, the butterfly *Oncidiums*, now better known as *Psychopsis*, that so influenced the Bachelor Duke. The spider orchids, *Brassias*, also fit into this group. Usually best in the greenhouse,

Right: *Colm.* Wildcat "Soroa Gato Rojo" is just one of the many clones of this hybrid. (AM/AOS)

breeders are developing strains that are more compact and easier to flower. These new types, including the species *Brs. verrucosa*, *Brs. longissima* and *Brs. gireoudiana*, are so free-flowering that they and their hybrids are developing into a new class of potted flowering plants. Showy is the only word that adequately describes a spray of one of these spidery blooms.

A continuing source of confusion for less well-read orchidists are the "true" miltonias from Brazil. Originally, the genus *Miltonia* comprised both the warmer growing Brazilian species with their distinctive spreading plants and the more compact mid-elevation Colombian types. As noted above, the Colombian and Peruvian species resembling pansies are now better known as *Miltoniopsis*, although their hybrids continue to be registered as miltonias. Even more confusing is the fact that very few hybrids between the two types have ever been successfully raised to flowering and fewer still remain in cultivation. In any case, *Milt. spectabilis*, and especially the variety Moreliana with its grape-purple blooms, is one of the most widely grown of the genus and is the basis of some wonderful warm-growing hybrids

Deserving of mention are two distinct growth habits common in the Oncidiinae. The first are the mule ear types, which have large, heavy, single leaves that may be 24in or more long and give long, rambling spikes of smallish blooms. These are orchids that require a lot of heat and high light to do well, but give an amazing show when well grown The most worthwhile species in this type include the longer-spiked types such as *Onc. carthaginense* and *Onc. luridum*, while shorter inflorescences are the norm in such popular types as *Onc. lanceanum* and *Onc. splendidum*. Long-lasting blooms in brilliant patterns or striking yellow make these spring bloomers highly in demand for orchid display work.

An almost diametrically opposed type in growth habit are the twig epiphytes, which are represented in more than a few Oncidiinae genera, and exploit a particular tropical niche. Light is often the limiting factor that determines where plants can and cannot grow in tropical forests. For

Left: *Fgtra.* Everglades Pioneer "Reverend Calvin Shave"—one of the very warmth-tolerant types developed in recent years. (AM/AOS)

this reason, plants that can grow where the light is available, such as in the perimeter of the forest or out on a limb in the twiggy outer growth of trees and shrubs, have an advantage over their peers. Equitant *Oncidiums* (or *Tolumnias*), *Comparettias*, *Rodriguezias*, *Ionopsis* and others exploit this niche with great success. These are fast-growing plants, and may be just as quick to die, if conditions do not suit them. Plants are often attached by only a few slender and precarious roots to thin, outer branches, where air circulation rapidly dries any accumulated moisture. Yet it is just these dainty plants that often prove the most popular in crowded windowsill collections, or for under-lights growers.

## The hybrids

Hybrids in the Oncidiinae illustrate just how closely all these many and varied genera and species really are, and how tenuous our grip on taxonomy remains. The classic definition of a species contains references to reproductively isolated and distinct populations. Yet in the Oncidiinae, as in other groups, what appear to be wildly differing flowers from widely separated areas will interbreed and produce fertile progeny. Moreover, hybrids are made not just between species presumably from the same genus, but species from different genera, making hybrids containing four, or five, or six or more genera in complex intergeneric combinations.

The complicated family tree of many *Oncidiums* and odonts is what makes their culture so difficult to generalize (more on this later). It is best to stay with our division into cooler and warmer growing types when discussing hybrids. As with the species, it is the cooler growing types based on *Odm. crispum* and *Odm. pescatorei*, as well as *Milt. vexillaria* and *Coch. noezliana*, that are the "queens" of the group with their beautiful sprays of widely patterned flowers and brilliance of color. Hybridizing in this group reached a peak between the two world wars that breeders now have only recently rescaled. Problems with aneuploidy (uneven chromosome counts that lead to poor growing and flowering) as well as with loss of genetic material in wartime Europe, set odont breeding back considerably. The studies of

Above: *Psychopsis* (**Oncidium**) *papilio* "Wanda" is a wonderful example of the species that "started it all" for the orchid hobby. (AM/AOS)

Above: *Onc.* (Geyser Gold x *macranthum*) is a hybrid from high elevation ***Oncidiums*** often segregated into the genus *Cyrtochilum*.

Dr. Don Wimber at the Eric Young Foundation in Jersey in the 1980s have resulted in tetraploid breeding stock in both odonts and *Miltoniopsis* that are enabling breeders to once again make fast progress with these plants.

However, it cannot be too strongly stressed just how difficult the high-elevation plants are to grow in most areas. Their main use today, especially with the newer tetraploids, is as parental stock to breed with warmer types to produce more temperature-tolerant hybrids that retain the brilliance and floriferous character of the *Odontoglossum* parent. Today we are seeing an entire range of hybrids such as *Colmanara* Wildcat that have all of the

Above: *Onc.* Lindsey Kone "Red Lip" represents the latest in equitant ***Oncidium*** breeding. (AM/AOS)

Left: *Onc.* (Geyser Gold x *macranthum*) is a hybrid from high elevation ***Oncidiums*** often segregated into the genus *Cyrtochilum*.

positive features of odont-type blooms on plants that are so much easier to grow and bloom. Indeed, these hybrids are forming the basis of an entirely new horticultural type that is proving itself on the potted plant market.

The potential for breeding does not stop with trying to recreate warmer odonts, either. Breeders are using odonts with more exotically shaped and patterned flowers to turn out whole new vistas in orchid flowers. When one goes beyond the *Odontocidiums* (*Odcdm.* = *Odontoglossum* x *Oncidium*), the *Wilsonaras* (*Wils.* = *Odontoglossum* x *Oncidium* x *Cochlioda*) and the *Colmanaras* (Colm. = *Odontoglossum* x *Miltonia* x *Oncidium*), the frontiers of

Oncidiinae breeding are reached. Here is where we see pioneering work with brassias to produce *Odontobrassias*, *Brassidiums*, *Maclellenaras*, and others that have the spidery "look" of the *Brassia* parent with the exotic color combinations of the *Odontoglossums*. *Miltassias* (*Mtssa.* = *Miltonia x Brassia*) have been especially productive in giving very warm-tolerant progeny with an array of colors and forms. Here is where it can get confusing, as it is the true Brazilian *Miltonias* such as *Milt. spectabilis* and *Milt. regnelii* that are used with *Brassias*, not the cooler growing Colombian "miltonias," the *Miltoniopsis*.

Nor should we ignore the many other fine hybrid groups within the Oncidiinae. For example, hybrids within *Brassia* attain levels of perfection that would not have been dreamt of 20 years ago. Today we see enormous "spiders" exceeding 16in in height, perfectly spaced on lightly arching stems, flowering on plants only a few years old. In years past, any *Brassia* that flowered was a "good" *Brassia*, owing to the difficulty in flowering many of the

Left: *Onc.* Nathakhun is a hybrid in the "mule-ear" group.

hybrids and species. Now we see them as potted flowering plants alongside *Dendrobiums* and *Phalaenopsis*.

*Miltonias*, both Brazilian and Colombian, form fascinating hybrid complexes. For the growers in warmer areas, the true *Miltonias* from Brazil come in wildly marked and exotically colored variety. Those who can provide more moderate to cool conditions can enjoy the vast range of the Colombian *Miltoniopsis* (known as "*Miltonias*" for hybrid registration purposes), in colors from purest white to deepest red with yellows and pinks in between, many with waterfall markings in the large lips. *Miltoniopsis* are among the most beautifully perfumed of all orchids, as well. The butterfly *Oncidiums*, now known as *Psychopsis*, include a range of hybrids that make easier-growing and larger examples of the typical species form. Equitant *Oncidiums*, or *Tolumnias*, so-called for their diminutive fan-shaped growths, are currently waxing in popularity. Inch-wide, round blooms are borne on upright spikes to a foot or more, and come in a range of color from white to yellow to red, many with brilliantly hued spotting on the prominent lips.

Above: *Wgfa.* Casseta "Everglades" is a multi-generic hybrid strongly influenced by brassia. (AM/AOS)

One of the most widely grown of all Oncidiinae is the dancing lady type. These have their basis both in *Onc. varicosum* and related Brazilian species, and in *Onc. sphacelatum*. *Onc. varicosum* hybrids have larger, more fully skirted, yellow blooms but may be more difficult for the beginner to grow, while the *Onc. sphacelatum* hybrids such as *Onc.* Gower Ramsey, have smaller blooms in much greater profusion and are much easier to grow. An orchid that has captured the fancy of the public if only because it has become nearly ubiquitous is *Onc.* Sharry Baby, an *Onc. ornithorhynchum* hybrid. With upright, branching spikes of medium size and rose-purple blooms, this plant's sheer ease of culture is matched only by its exquisite fragrance.

## The care

In a group as diverse as the Oncidiinae, it is valuable to try to find some common ground. Unfortunately, there is little to be found! Many in the group will do quite well in a potting mix similar to that used for *Paphiopedilums*. One widely used media is a combination of well-screened fine fir bark, coarse charcoal, and sponge-rock, in proportions of roughly 3:1:1. However, there are those that will do better in a slightly coarser mix more similar to that appropriate for *Phalaenopsis* or *Cattleyas*. These plants tend to be those that are larger, with coarser roots. Plants from drier locations are also happier in a faster-draining mix. Finally, there are those, notably the twig epiphytes, that just will not do well unless grown on a mount of cork or hardwood. This group wants to be watered often, but must dry quickly and completely between waterings. A greenhouse is almost a

Left: *Mtssa.* Pelican Lake "Everglades" is a similar hybrid with strong brassia influence. (HCC/AOS)

Below: *Helcia sanguinolenta* is an obscure species in the ***Oncidium*** group.

necessity for such plants to ensure adequate humidity. Only a very few of the high-elevation species will require any special care, such as sphagnum moss, which is famous for growing plants that won't grow any other way.

As with media, there are some generalities to be found in temperature ranges. Many of the most commonly grown species and hybrids will do quite well under *Cattleya* conditions of 55–60°F nights and 80°F days. If days can be kept under 90°F and a good temperature differential provided, the range of plants available to the grower is even wider, as the coolish night temperature seems to be a critical factor in keeping plants happy. There are, of course, the cool

Above: *Milt. phalaenopsis* is the species that has given us the popular "waterfall" hybrids.

types that will not survive unless the days are kept well under 80°F and the nights go into the 50s°F. Good air circulation and ventilation will help to keep temperatures in check. Colombian *Miltonias*, or *Miltoniopsis*, are not quite "cool" growers, but resent temperature extremes. Growers will obtain the best results when nights are in the lower 60s°F and the days do not go much above 80°F. Some of the more tropical types will require higher temperatures, but these are the exceptions.

Light and temperature go together. The most satisfactory method of moderating temperature is to ensure that light levels do not go higher than the plants' needs. In general, the harder and tougher the plant's foliage, the more light it will require to do well, and the higher the temperature it can stand. Alternately, the thinner and more delicate the leaves, the more sensitive the plant will be to bright light and high temperatures. Most *Oncidiums* and odonts will do best with light levels slightly less than for cattleyas, but slightly more than for paphs or phals. If temperatures can be kept in check with cooling or ventilation, light levels can be higher, which can often give more flowers.

Many Oncidiinae respond to higher light levels by a reddening of the foliage; this is not unlike tanning in humans. Depending on the type, this may or may not be a favorable symptom, though if only a slight reddening is visible, this usually means the plant is getting all the light it can use and this will result in better flower production. Plants receiving insufficient light will be dark green and very soft, often with leaves that will not support themselves. Such plants will rarely flower satisfactorily, if at all. The best time to move plants like this back into higher light conditions is during winter, when the sunlight is at a lower level—this will allow the plant to acclimatize gradually as the days lengthen and the light gets stronger. It is not unlike your first day at the beach after a long winter.

Above: *Milt.* Dainty Miss is an excellent example of modern use of *Milt. phalaenopsis* as a parent.

Most Oncidiinae prefer to be evenly

moist, with the notable exception of some of the harder-leafed plants that should be treated like *Cattleyas*. In general, the higher the elevation from which the plant (or its parents) originates, the more important good quality water will be. Good quality water will be low in dissolved solids and of nearly neutral pH. Water "softened" with sodium chloride (common table salt) should never—without exception—be used on any plant. Poor root growth and burned leaf tips are symptoms of poor quality water.

An unseen disadvantage to poor water is the resultant poor root growth that will make the plant less able to stand up to other adverse environmental problems, especially heat. This is most notable in *Miltoniopsis* grown in areas where the temperature regime may be marginal. Plants grown with good quality water will have good root systems that can support the plant in

Left: *Odm. lindenii* is a rare, high elevation species.

stressful times, while those grown with poor water will show a decline under less-than-favorable conditions. It is especially important to use the "weakly, weekly" system of fertilizing members of this group to avoid the potential of salt buildup and root loss.

Breeders are concentrating not only on flower quality in the Oncidiinae. They are looking for plants that grow quickly and flower easily under a variety of conditions. This is to the hobbyists' advantage, as such plants will often do quite well for them, too. However, it is important to recognize that plants grown for commercial purposes are grown under optimal conditions and may take some time to settle in before performing well for their new owners. This will be especially noticeable in many odont types. Make an extra effort to keep your flowering plants in a cool and moist area after purchase, rather than right in front of the furnace or air conditioner, or on

Right: *Onc. onustum*, by contrast, is a lowland species requiring lots of sun and high temperatures to do well.

*Oda.* Mem. Kendrick Williams

Above: *Milt.* (Melissa Baker x *phalaenopsis*) illustrates more current work with the species parent.

Right: *Oda.* Picotee "Peppermint"—well illustrates why many consider the Colombian *Odm. crispum*-based hybrids to be among the most beautiful of all orchids. They are, unfortunately, difficult to grow in all but the most consistently cool of climates.

top of the television. The large spikes produced by these plants places quite a strain on them, especially in stressful environments, so careful placement in their first few weeks with you will pay dividends later.

# PAPHIOPEDILUM OR THE SLIPPER ORCHIDS

No other orchid, indeed few other plants, are so treasured by collectors as are members of the slipper orchid group: *Cypripediums*, *Paphiopedilums*, *Phragmipediums* and the rarely cultivated *Selenipediums*, which are among the world's tallest orchids. *Cypripediums* generally inhabit more temperate zones and, until very recently, have been considered nearly impossible to grow in cultivation. These will not be a topic, nor will the never-seen *Selenipediums*, which as reedy plants growing to 10ft or taller with ephemeral blooms, have not been the focus of any horticultural interest. The slipper orchids that have captured and held the imaginations—not to mention pocketbooks—of collectors for well over 100 years are the New World *Phragmipediums* and the Old World *Paphiopedilums*. They are characterized by the lip being modified into a pouch- or slipper-like structure that functions in the pollination mechanism. Most slipper orchids also have the ventral sepals joined into one, rather than two distinct, as with many orchids. Another character that sets this group apart from most other commonly seen orchids is the unique column structure.

Paphiopedilums, or paphs, represent some of the most highly priced orchids ever traded, and until recently, were much more sought-after than their generally plainer New World cousins, *Phragmipediums*, or phrags. The discovery

Above: *Paph.* Herbert Bernhard "Joyce Kelly" is exemplary of the renewed interest multiflora paphs. (HCC/AOS)

of one species, *Phrag. besseae*, in the early 1980s, is all it took to launch phrags into the center of intense amateur and commercial interest.

The story of *Phrag. besseae* can serve as a modern morality tale of the entire group of slipper orchids. The few plants initially discovered, and the plant's bright orange-red blooms, led the discoverers to believe that the species was rare. After all, how could such a showy thing have been overlooked? As more and more searching was done in similar habitats it was rather quickly found that *besseae* was not so rare as first thought. In addition, growers began to make self and sibling crosses to raise plants from seed, increasing the available quantity. Hybrids joined the species, adding to the knowledge of how quickly and easily the species and its hybrids could be produced in cultivation, particularly when aided by colchicine conversion to tetraploidy.

Today, wild-collected plants have difficulty selling at even moderate prices, and hybrids that once brought hundreds of dollars can be found for $20. Nor is this situation unique to *Phrag. besseae* and its hybrids. The same sort of thing happened with many others such as—to name just two—*Paph. rothschildianum* and vinicolor (wine-colored) *Paph. maudiaes*.

Above: *Paph. concolor* is one of the easiest members of its group to grow. It was formerly known as *Brachypetalum* but now properly *Concoloria*.

Since the mid-19th century, when paphs first began to be seen in Western collections, they have had their fanatic adherents. In those very early days, their culture was little understood, and they had to suffer through the same stove house treatment given other "tropical" plants. When this

insult was added to the injury often suffered in the long transit back from their collection sites in India, Burma, China, or other Asian locales, it is little wonder why the paphs retained their rare status well into the later part of the century.

The first paph to flower in European collections was the famously easy-to-grow *Paph. venustum* in the U.K. in 1819. Other species followed as collectors were sent out to recently discovered, or at least recently pacified, areas.

However, just because a species was discovered and entered into cultivation did not guarantee its permanent place in horticulture. Collectors were vague at best, and dissembling at worst, when giving accurate information about the locale of the plants they had gathered. Understandably, growers find it very difficult to cultivate a plant well without accurate habitat information. This, coupled with notoriously poor growing techniques, led to some wonderful plants being "lost" for considerable time after their initial discovery. Two prime

Above: *Paph. henryanum* is one of the newer Chinese paph species.

Left: *Paph. spicerianum* is a very nice species and instrumental in the production of our modern "bulldog" paph hybrids.

examples are *Paph. fairrieanum* and *Paph. sanderianum*. *Paph. fairrieanum* was first flowered in the English collection of Mr. Fairrie in 1857. The supply of plants dwindled until few or no known examples remained in cultivation, resulting in the posting of a £1,000 bounty for the rediscovery of the species—which remained unclaimed until nearly 50 years later in 1905. The story of the long-petalled *Paph. sanderianum*, described in 1886, is even more extreme, with some growers doubting that the plant had ever really existed. Its habitat was finally discovered exactly a hundred years later in 1986.

In nature, paphs are primarily terrestrial, with only five known epiphytes: *Paph. parishii*, *lowii*, *villosum*, *glanduliferum*, and *hirsutissimum*. Their habitats range from sea level to over 7,546ft. and from India east across south China, southeast Asia, Malaysia, New Guinea, and the Solomon Islands. Many inhabit areas where dappled light is the rule, and deep shade is often the case. A few of the multiflora strap-leaf types do, however, grow in sunlight and require higher light to do well, but in general, paphs are shade-loving plants.

The substrates that most often host paphs tend to retain an even level of moisture, while not remaining saturated. An apt comparison would be with the duffy humus that forms on the floor of a temperate zone deciduous forest. Indeed, oak leaf mold formed an important constituent of media used prior to and right after World War 2. The sort of shady habitat of many paphs can easily be duplicated in the home, making paphs one of the best house plant orchids, if the type is properly selected. Not all paphs, especially certain species and their hybrids, are equally easy to grow or adaptable to home conditions. Fortunately, the types most often encountered by beginners are easy to grow and adaptable just by the fact that they've been in mass production.

## The species

Happily, Paphiopedilum species sort out nicely into a series of groups with generally related flower forms and culture. Although

Right: *Paph. esquirolei* "Amy Brook" is a species that is often confused with the similar *Paph. hirsutissimum*. (HCC/AOS)

Above: *Paph. philippenense* is a variable species much used in hybridizing.

modern breeders have created many intersectional hybrids, still more are made each year that are within the particular group, making knowledge of the various sections vital to the successful care of your plants.

## The *Barbata* section

The first orchid, at least the first slipper orchid, for many will be a species or hybrid from the *Barbata* section. There is much to recommend this group, with their beautifully marbled foliage, tall stems, and wide range of colors. The species after which this section is named, *Paph. barbatum*, is typical with its purple-veined white dorsal, brownish-purple pouch, matching the petals held proudly over nicely patterned foliage. Similar to *Paph. barbatum*, with larger petals held at a slightly lower angle, is *Paph. callosum*, one of the most widespread and important of all paph species. *Paph. callosum* is one of the easiest to grow, too, coexisting quite happily with phals, or as one of your higher light houseplants. Other species of note in this group are *Paph. superbiens*, *lawrenceanum*, *hennisianum*, *acmodontum* and *sukhakulii*. These species make very satisfactory potted plants, and each grows pretty much like the other. There is an entire range of hybrids from this section known as Maudiae types, which will be discussed later.

Above: *Paph. tigrinum* "Nike" is another rather newly discovered paph species. (HCC/AOS)

## Multiflora strap-leaf types

Two of the previously referenced "mythic" slippers are members of the *Coryopedilum* section, better known as the multiflora strap-leaf types. For the sake of convenience, we'll treat most of the paphs with multiple flowers all together here, though they are placed botanically in several sections including *Pardalopetalum* and

Left: *Paph. bellatulum* album "JEM" was once extremely rare and considered among the most difficult of all paphs to grow. Today, thanks to seed culture and strict selection, plants are easier to grow and more commonly available, though still expensive. (AM/AOS)

*Cochlopetalum*. The members of *Cochlopetalum*, including *glaucophyllum* and *victoria-mariae*, are sequentially flowering, that is, bear two or three flowers at a time over a long period. Some plants have been known to give 30-plus flowers over a year or more. *Cochlopetalums* require a bit more shade and moisture than do their simultaneous flowering cousins.

It is in the multiflora group that some of the most enthusiasm has been found in the last 20 years. The rediscovery of the habitat of *sanderianum* and *rothschildianum*, as well as their successful culture from seed-raised populations, has led to a burst of hybridizing. Of course, when growers are making a lot of hybrids, a lot of plants are grown, leading to lower prices and increased availability. Some of the showiest of all paph species are found here, including the two previously named, as well as *philippenense*, *lowii*, *haynaldianum*, *adductum*, *stonei*, and *praestans*, among others. Strap-leaf types require higher light and heat to do well than do some paphs, and take somewhat longer to mature to flowering size. Repotting or dividing can also slow the plants' progress to flowering, so must be done only as necessary and with great care.

## Standard Hybrids

Section *Paphiopedilum* contains the species upon which are based modern "standard" hybrids, including *insigne*, *villosum* (including

Right: *Paph.* Lady Isabel has multiple stately blooms borne over handsome strap-leafed foliage.

Above: *Paph.* Red Glory "Rockwell's Orchids" is exemplary of the new vini ("wine") color paphs. (HCC/AOS)

*boxalli*), and *spicerianum*. Plants in this section have plain green leaves that are somewhat softer than those of the strap-leaf group, generally preferring more shade and moisture as well. *Paph. insigne*, particularly, makes a very nice plant to grow simply because it is so prolific and easy, and comes in a variety of colors—from bronzy tones with spots to pure green or yellow. *Insigne* was a standard cut flower for many years. Its sister species also make good potted plants, and are often very compact, especially *spicerianum* and *charlesworthii*. *Paph. fairrieanum* is another of the most charming paph species, with an oriental look. All of these species found homes in the conservatories of Victorian England, where they favored their owners with a profusion of blooms on tallish straight stems during the winter into spring.

## *Concoloria* and *Parvisepalum* section

We have saved for last what many orchid enthusiasts consider to be the most beautiful of all orchids, and nearly all agree are among the most difficult to grow well. Formerly all together in the *Brachypetalum* section, recent discoveries in China of related species have led to reclassification into two groups, *Concoloria* and *Parvisepalum*. Even though split into two, it is easy to see the close relationship between these two sections in the flowers, which are generally in tones not found in other sections of the genus, and in the plants, which are also highly characteristic.

*Concoloria* species have round flowers ranging in color from white, often with some degree of spotting, through cream to yellow, on generally short stems. The plants are often smaller than most other paph types, with hard leaves mottled to varying degrees with silvery tones. The most commonly seen species are *bellatulum*, *concolor*, *niveum* and *godefroyae*. The pink paph, *delanatii*, from Vietnam, was included in this group by default until the opening of mainland China in the 1980s led to the discovery of an entire range of species heretofore unexpected.

As species like *armeniacum*, with its brilliant yellow blooms, *micranthum*, *malipoense*, and *emersonii* began to emerge, it became clear that these species formed a natural group and such was constituted as *Parvisepalum*. Plants are generally similar to, though larger, than those in *Concoloria*; while flowers are in hues unseen in paphs such as raspberry, deep green and pink. Hybridizing continues to proceed at a furious pace to see what this brand-new group of species can produce.

### Phragmipedium species

These can be treated as a group, although they, too, are broken down further into section. Some of the most popularly seen are *longifolium*, probably the easiest to grow; *caudatum*, with its petals that can reach 36in; *schlimii*, one of the prettiest of pinks; a group of species clustering around *ecuadorense*; and the newly discovered orange *besseae*. Most of these tropical American species grow in association with moisture, whether in actual seepage, along streambeds or in constantly moist areas like the clay in a road cut. For this reason, most phrags do best when kept evenly moist—some even preferring to be kept sitting in water, a no-no for most orchids—and seldom disturbed by potting or dividing.

### The hybrids

No other genus has sustained the same level of hybridizing interest over the past 150 years. A recent count showed that 10,000 of approximately 100,000 registered hybrids were in *Paphiopedilum*—an astonishing 10 percent! The value and longevity of this group of orchids is best shown by the fact that the first hybrid to flower in the genus, *Paph. harrisianum* (*villosum x barbatum*), flowered and was awarded in 1869. It is still in widespread cultivation and is in fair demand. The Vietch nursery named it "Dr. Harris" after the man who first suggested to their grower, John Dominy, how to pollinate orchids.

Thankfully, none but the specialist needs to know any more than a little about the various lines of breeding, and then only insofar as it affects the care of the plants. Until the last ten years or so, the most popular types were the so-called bulldog or toad paphs bred from the members of the *Paphiopedilum* section. These were the most highly developed over the years, based largely in *Paph. Leeanum* (*insigne x spicerianum*) and resultant polyploid cultivars. Robust green-leafed plants give rise to sturdy stems of single, round flowers of large size and surprising color combinations ranging from pure green to deep red to densely spotted. Toads take some getting used to, but are among the most satisfying and long-lasting of all orchids.

However, today's buyers are more liable to first run across a Maudiae-type paph. Bred largely from members of the barbata, no other paph has satisfied so many for so many years. *Paph. Maudiae* was first registered in 1900 as the albino (green and white) hybrid between *lawrenceanum* and *callosum*. A *coloratum* version soon followed, with the most richly colored of this hybrid going on to breed an entire race of bright hybrids. Today, we have the green Maudiaes, the coloratum, flames, peacocks, and vinicolors, all resulting from different color forms of the parental species. Into this mix have been added the other members of the section, and we also see Maudiae types contributing to a brand new color range when the vinicolors are crossed with standard (*insigne*-based) types.

Excitement also runs high for strap leaf multiflora hybrids. When several different artificially raised populations of *rothschildianum* began to flower in the late 1970s and early 1980s, breeders took advantage of the previously rare opportunity to use this species as a parent.

As a result access to hybrids, once only available as divisions of mature plants at elevated prices, became much easier and less expensive as seedling of various sizes became available. *Paph.* St. Swithin (*rothschildianum x philippenense*), Julius (*roths. x lowii*), Lady Isabel (*roths. x stonei*), and Susan Booth (*roths. x praestans*), among so many others, became almost common, although retaining their worth as the best of the type.

Just about every imaginable combination of species within this group has been tried. Some are good; some are not so good, giving the worst of their parents rather than the best. Breeders have also made outcrosses with members of other sections, notably the Maudiae types that make good hybrids generally, and with an assortment of the brachys which can be either very good or awful. The danger with this sort of disparate breeding is that progeny can occasionally be difficult or impossible to flower.

Of course, if paph lovers adore white and pink paphs even more, then it is only natural that hybrids in this group would be highly sought-after. *Paph.* Vanda M. Pearman (*delanatii x bellatulum*) and Psyche (*niveum x bellatulum*) are just two examples of the fine and uniform hybrids that can be made using *Concoloria*, either with other

Above: *Phrag.* Grande "Nuuanu"—one of the most popular of the New World slipper hybrids. (HCC/AOS)

species in the section, or with members of the *Parvis*. The 1990s saw an explosion of this type, both in quantity and in quality. We can be grateful that they are, in general, easier to grow than the species. As with the strap leaf multifloras, intersectional crosses are also attempted and are rather speculative. However, when the breeder is lucky, as in *Paph.* Po Tree (*malipoense* x Yellow Tree), or good, as in Skip Bartlett (*godefroyae* x F.C. Puddle), individual clones of great merit will arise (Po Tree) as well as a breakthrough in further white breeding (Skip Bartlett.)

## The care

There are a few generalities that apply throughout the slipper orchids. The first is that none of them like full sun for any part of the day. All are from more-or-less forested or shaded habitats and will burn if exposed to light that is too strong. How strong is too strong? This depends on the type; plants with mottled foliage, as in the Maudiae types and the white paphs, tend to do best in the same sort of light regime that *Phalaenopsis* enjoy. The

Left: *Phrag.* Mem. Dick Clements "66th St."—when *Phrag. besseae* burst onto the scene in the early 1980s, it began a revolution in phrag breeding that is still playing out. (AM/AOS)

same sort of light conditions will suit the bulldog types, though in neither of these instances will the grower want to see leaves of dark green. Rather the leaves should be medium green stiff, not limp. The exception to this rule is the strap-leaf types, which will require stronger light to grow and flower well. With the stronger light will come naturally higher temperatures. A light regime as for *Cattleya*s might be too strong, but not by much. Successful growers often use hanging plants of this group to shade their more shade-loving plants. The leaves should be medium green and held horizontally, not limply.

Almost no slipper orchid will tolerate dry medium. Plants are accustomed to an evenly moist substrate in nature and this is what suits them best in cultivation. Along with this goes a real sensitivity to salinity and dissolved solids in the soil solution. If the plants are allowed to dry too much and/or for too long, the solids will concentrate to a point where root death will occur. The single most important factor in the growth of healthy paphs is good quality water. For this same reason, paphs—with the exception of the strap-leaf multifloras—are not heavy feeders. The best practice is to feed at one-quarter or less strength each week, alternating once a month with a thorough flushing with clean water. The medium should be able to hold both air and water, as well.

Although paph species inhabit a wide elevational range, most will live in the same temperature range. The best plants seem to be grown in an environment that maintains a bit of the day's warmth into the night—no lower than 55–60° at night, and day's heating with sunlight into the low 80s°F. This moderate temperature range will give the healthiest plants, with the least stress, and consequently the best flower. Again, the strap-leaf types are the exception, requiring slightly warmer conditions to do their best, along with a greater day-night differential in late winter to initiate flowering. Plants grown toward the cooler end of the range will be easier to manage, while those grown toward the warmer end may need increased fertilizer and water, which can give soft growth that is susceptible to rot. If such rot is seen (and it needs to be stressed that in no other orchid is good sanitation so important)

Above: *Paph. charlesworthii* is a pretty and compact species that is becoming increasingly important as a parent.

remove the leaf at the base and allow air to reach the wound for healing.

Good quality light, proper watering, and air movement will go a long way toward helping your plants to do their best. One last word, a paph needs a good root system. While the roots will never be extensive in the same way other orchids' might, a strong system of roots will help your plants to succeed. High quality water low in dissolved solids, light feeding, and proper watering practices will ensure your plants have the sort of roots that will carry them through the inevitable times of stress.

# PHALAENOPSIS

For a group of orchids that is today nearly ubiquitous, *Phalaenopsis* (or phals) did not enjoy the initial rapid popularity of other genera such as *Cattleya* and *Paphiopedilum*. While phals were among the earliest orchids described in Europe, living, flowering examples did not begin to be seen until the middle of the 19th century. It is relatively easy to understand why botanists would chance upon such a showy plant early in the exploration of the Old World tropics, with the sprays of lovely white blooms swaying gently in the breeze. The first phal to be described was *Phal. amabilis* in 1750,

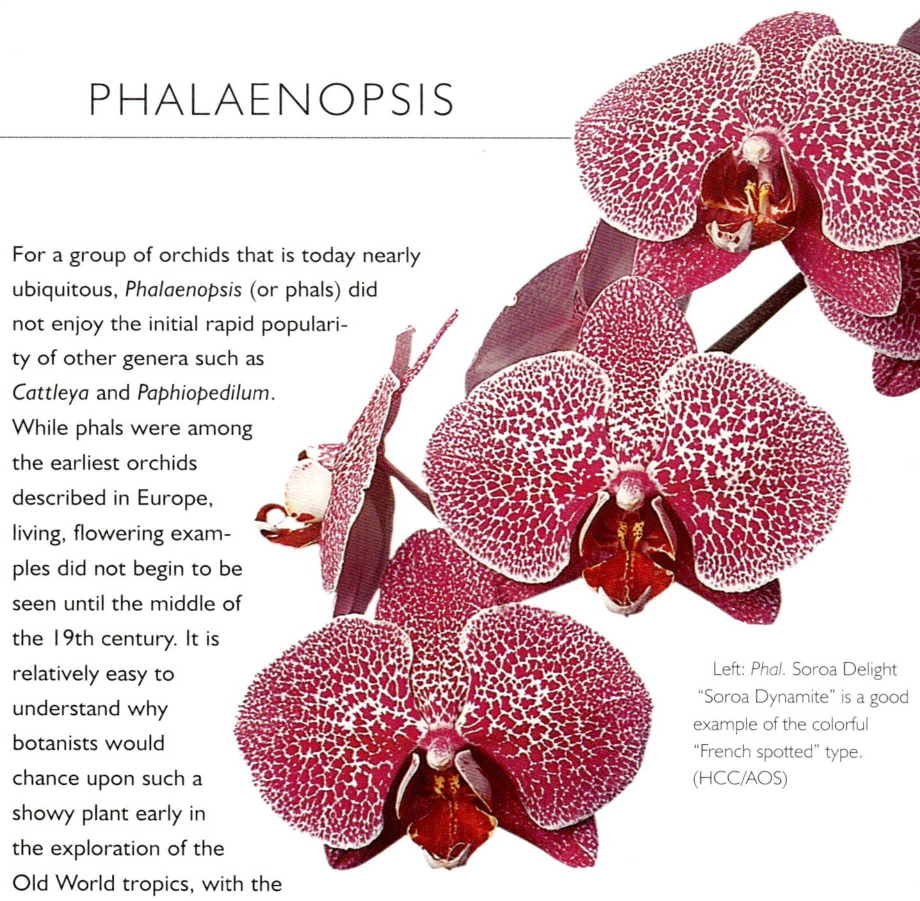

Left: *Phal.* Soroa Delight "Soroa Dynamite" is a good example of the colorful "French spotted" type. (HCC/AOS)

Right: *Phal. schilleriana* is among the most beautiful of all orchids, with cascades of soft rose-pink blooms and beautifully patterned foliage.

though it was first known as *Angraecum album majus* ("Angraek" means orchid in Malay). It was not transferred to the newly created genus *Phalaenopsis* as the type species until 1825.

Discovery of new species followed at a plodding pace, with *Phal. aphrodite* the first to arrive in the U.K. in 1837, followed by *Phal. equestris* in 1840, *Phal. schilleriana* in 1858 and *stuartiana* not until 1881.

Below: *Phal. stuartiana* "Susanna" is closely related to *schilleriana*, and is the source of most of our modern spotted hybrids. It shares *schilleriana*'s beautiful foliage. (HCC/AOS)

*Doritis pulcherrima*, a closely related genus thought by some taxonomists to belong to *Phalaenopsis* rather than a separate genus, was first described in 1833. Though the species were being collected and described, it should not be construed—unlike in some other genera—that initial importations or attempts to grow phals were successful. Indeed, even though *aphrodite* was introduced into England in 1837, it is noted as first flowering in 1847, nearly ten years later. Extremely slow transportation modes from the very distant South Pacific areas were certainly the main culprits, as phals lack the water storage capabilities of many other pseudobulbous orchids. The slow growth of popularity of these orchids must be viewed alongside the difficulty in propagating the plants, as their long spikes of moth-like blooms must have made them much in demand.

Right: *Phal. aphrodite* "Plantation" is among the most developed of species. This one is probably a seventh or eighth generation sibling cross. (HCC/AOS)

Phals are monopodial, growing straight up (for a more complete description of the monopodial habit, see *Vandas*) generally with broad thin leaves on very short, usually unbranched, stems. The leaves easily dehydrate, and plants are very difficult to rescue in European type climates owing to lack of adequate heat and humidity. Even today, phals arriving from overseas after a trip of only a week or less, often are flattened in the boxes like pancakes, and can be slow to recover if imported in the wrong season.

It is easy to see, therefore, how *Phalaenopsis* presented a particular challenge to Victorian orchid growers. Nevertheless, early orchid literature is replete with descriptions and engravings depicting large, mature plants of such showy species as *Phal. amabilis*, *aphrodite*, and *schilleriana* growing robustly in hanging baskets, flowering profusely in their mid-winter season. This extravagance was not without its cost. Victorian-era greenhouses

were profligate with their heating, necessary to the well-being of tropical species facing a typically dreary English winter, and manpower, needed to take each of the sometimes hundreds of baskets down for their periodic tank dippings which served to water the plants. The practice of dipping phals, rather than watering from the top with a hose, persisted in some cases well into the years between the wars, as it was felt (rightly so) that these were more-than-usually susceptible to crown rot if water was allowed to lodge in the growing point of the plant. With the dim and cold conditions of English and European establishments, this was certainly the case, and it took several decades of confidence-building by American growers, benefiting from a more friendly climate, to depart from accepted practices.

Only with the initiation of fir-bark based culture, with its better drainage, and improved light and air movement, did growers begin to grow confidently on benches. Antiquated practices kept phals from showing their true value as horticultural subjects until relatively recently, when technology began to be exercised to get seedlings growing to their maximum rate and, hence, lowest cost. With this improved

Left: *Phal.* Maritea "Lesa's Galaxy" shows the advances in modern novelty types, especially in brilliance of color and distinct patterning. (HCC/AOS)

Above: *Dtps. Mem.* Dr. Ho "Roman Holiday." (HCC/AOS.)

technology, phals have become big business around the world, giving lush floral displays for a minimum of cost and effort, at least for an orchid! They have truly become nearly ubiquitous.

Ubiquitous is not too strong a word, especially in the United States, where the production of *Phalaenopsis* pot plants far outstrips even that of their closest competitor, *Dendrobiums*. Whether the plants are produced entirely in domestic nurseries, or simply locally finished imported examples, the fact remains the rapidly growing U.S. market is consuming more than ten million flowering *Phalaenopsis* annually. More than

Right: *Phal. equestris* is another species highly prized and developed by generations of in-breeding.

Above: *Phal.* Cassandra "Tammy Lee" is a modern remake of one of the first registered *Phalaenopsis* hybrids. (HCC/AOS)

one million square feet of nursery space in Florida, California, and Texas, as well as less in other states, are devoted to these obviously profitable plants. Until the mid-1980s, most *Phalaenopsis* production continued to adhere to a production time approaching four years, from seed to flowering. Such long production times are simply not profitable to growers for the mass market.

With the market for flowering potted plants finally blossoming in the U.S., growers of other potted plants—notably *bromeliads*, *spathiphyllums*, and *anthuriums*—began to experiment with techniques that would allow them to significantly reduce the traditional production time. This experimentation came more-or-less simultaneously with offshore producers reaching a saturation point with their established markets and a consequent need to find new markets. What has 250 million consumers and not enough flowers? That's right . . . the United States.

The third ingredient needed to spur the rapid rise of phals as America's number four flowering potted plant was a vast merchandising effort by mass marketers through the so-called "Big Boxes" like Home Depot and Lowes Viola! Production, distribution (through established channels to the Big Boxes along with other flowering plants) and big sales. Plants that would have cost $30, $40, $50, or more even ten years ago are available for $19.95, with a result that is profoundly altering the hobbyist orchid world.

### The species

Phal species are among the loveliest of all orchids. Best-known are the species in the *Euphalaenopsis*, or true *Phalaenopsis*, though the *stauroglottis*—star-shaped—species have a long-lasting decorative appeal exceeded only by their hybrids. *Euphalaenopsis* species include the white *amabilis* and *aphrodite*, the spotted white *stuartiana*, and the lovely pink *schilleriana*. The last two species have wonderfully silver-marbled foliage, while the first two have solid green leaves. Also included here, if only on an honorary basis, is the miniature species *equestris*, which has proven to be so valuable in the breeding of potted plant types. All of these species, except *equestris*, share the characteristic of having flowers relatively large in proportion to the plant and spike habit. Upright, arching inflorescenses are the rule, and are often branching; though *schilleriana* especially may be nearly pendant if left unstaked. From these five species have come nearly all of the important traits of our pastel modern standard hybrids.

Also, in no other genus has more line breeding of species been done to such great affect. Because phals grow relatively fast, even under less-than-ideal conditions, several generations can be packed into less time than it might take to grow and flower one generation of a *Cattleya* or *Cymbidium* or *Vanda*. Today, when these phal species are offered for sale, it can be safely assumed that they are seed-raised from selected parents. Especially in *equestris* and *aphrodite*, the improvement over the typical species is startling.

Less appealing to the untrained eye are the *stauroglottis* species, including, but not limited to, *violacea*, *amboinensis*, *lueddemanniana*, *mannii* and *venosa*. There are over a dozen other species in this group of lesser horticultural importance. The five named have particular beauty, aside from their importance in the creation of brighter and more unusual colors in hybrids. None have the wonderfully decorative flowering habit of the *Euphalaenopsis*, though mature plants can and will produce multiple inflorescence (it is unusual for most *Euphalaenopsis* to produce more than a couple or three spikes at a time) of brightly colored and sometimes perfumed blooms.

*Phal. violacea* is the shyest to produce flowers, though its green and rose blooms are sweetly scented, and the foliage is broad and shiny. *Phal. amboinensis* makes slightly longer inflorescences and more flowers, often cream or yellow with mahogany banding. *Phal. lueddemanniana* has brilliant magenta barring in the best forms, while *Phal. mannii* is notable for its rich yellow blooms. Lastly, *venosa* (a more recently popular species) has two main color ranges, one browner and one more yellow, but both of which have proven invaluable in further breeding.

Whether or not *Doritis* is a valid genus is best left up to the taxonomists. The effect of a name change would be felt, especially at first, only in the circles of the most intensely interested, as there are too many *Doritaenopsis* (*Dtps.* = *Doritis* x *Phalaenopsis*) to simply wish away, even though modern breeders believe that there may actually be less *Doritis* influence in our present-day *Dtps.* than even genealogical analysis might suggest. The plants of *Doritis* certainly appear to be much like those of phals, even if their habit is more likely to be lithophytic or terrestrial, and the leaves are often stiffer and more upright. The strictly upright, occasionally branching inflorescences bear medium sized blooms of rich magenta to softer pink. The flowers tend to be paler, as well as larger, and are often placed into a separate species or variety, *buysonniana*.

Thai breeders have gone a long way with different forms of this species, producing even more brilliant fuchsia, purer whites and a range of peloric (where the petals resemble the lip to a greater or lesser

Above: *Phal. Venimp* "Carib" is a colorful and fragrant primary hybrid. (HCC/AOS)

extent) combinations. These same breeders have begun to use the brilliant fuchsia blooms to produce a range of intergenerics including vandaceous genera. *Doritis* is also valuable in hybridizing as it flowers in summer, and changes the season of phals (with which it is bred) more toward the spring from the normal winter season.

## The hybrids

To describe the entire range of *Phalaenopsis* hybrids easily available today would take an entire book. The broad spectrum of colors, patterns, and sizes provide a textbook example of persistence and insight on the part of breeders from Taiwan, the U.S., France, and Germany. The palette of color ranges from purest, sparkling white, through soft pinks and lavender, to richer roses and magenta, to boldly striped or spotted, white or lavender, through to brilliant, sunny yellows and golds, and on to near reds and purples, as well as the occasional blue. Size can vary from less than one inch to nearly six inches, and the flower count from a few to dozens.

It is almost hard to believe how much breeders have balanced the array of available characters, and in some cases used mutations from the meristem process for characters previously unavailable. But a balance it is—trading size and shape for color intensity, and so on back and forth.

Right: *Phal.* Golden Gift "Roman Holiday" was commended for its unusually marked petals, which mimic the lip in a mutation known as "peloric." (JC/AOS)

Above: *Phal. amabilis* "David Taylor," often confused with *aphrodite*. It has been almost as extensively inbred as *aphrodite* and *equestris*. (AM/AOS)

The smaller-flowered species, with their generally brighter colors, have contributed the depth of pigmentation, while larger-flowered types have given the full shape and floriferous character demanded by decorators.

Most of us are used to the yearly introductions of new garden annuals and perennials, but few enthusiasts would have expected orchids to have been so commonplace as to see vases of stunning cut-flowers in the homes shown in glossy magazines. Yet it is hybrid *Phalaenopsis* that have made orchids into the enormously popular crop that they have become today. The next time you see a photo spread on a celebrity's home and you see orchids, the chances are that it is a hybrid phal, and a plant that you, too, could have on your coffee table, in the color combination of your choice. And what is best about this scenario—with the color, the display, and the affordable cost? It is that you, who cannot justify buying a plant or plants for a onetime display, can grow phals in your home and reflower them year after year with a minimum of effort.

## The care

Unlike *Cattleyas* or *Vandas*, which represent two other frequently cited culture regimes, *Phalaenopsis* are shade-loving plants and will grow, as well as flower, very nicely in a well-lit home. Indeed, if you have any success at all with other flowering houseplants, such as African violets, you will find phals to be easy. Phals will grow better in a greenhouse or a sunroom, of course, but it is not necessary, as has been found by windowsill growers from crowded Europe and Japan, to the big cities of the U.S. An eastern window is ideal, though a shaded south or west window will also produce satisfactory results. The most important factor to remember is that the broad leaves of these plants will burn easily if exposed to too much sunlight. If the leaves are warm to the touch, light or heat buildup needs to be addressed. Heat buildup can be caused by bright light, but is also a factor of inadequate air movement, which allows air and leaves to overheat. Phals are also excellent subjects for growing under lights: there are plenty of more compact types that will give nearly the floral impact for less than half the space of a traditional hybrid.

The most critical factor, after light, for home care is the provision of adequate (40% or more) humidity. This is most easily accomplished by growing plants in a group, which allows the collective transpiration to produce a more humid microclimate. This also allows the grower to use other plants as temporary shading, to provide higher light nearer the light source to those that require it, while they protect the delicate types in their shadow. Watering is much easier when the plants are grouped together: this can often be accommodated by growing the plants in watertight trays that are drained by means of a normally plugged spigot and hose.

Because they are tropical plants, used to the warmth and humidity of the forest, phals are intolerant of dryness in the atmosphere or in the pot. Plants want to be kept evenly moist. This is a difficult concept for many beginners, who tend to interpret it as "keep wet." "Evenly moist" means to never allow the medium to dry completely, to water it once a day or so before it has time to dry out. This is best judged by periodically picking up the pots, which will easily give their water content by their changing weight. Phals that are allowed to dry out too thoroughly will usually respond in the same way that overwatered plants will, they will lose their roots and become dehydrated. With higher watering needs, and faster growth, come increased fertilizer needs. Fertilize with a product appropriate to your medium at one-half strength every week, and your plants will thank you.

Repotting phals is an easy task, and generally should be performed each year, in the spring months right after flowering when new roots emerge from the base of the stem. (For a closer look at this, see illustrations in the chapter on "Growing Orchids at Home.") If you pot regularly, you need not overpot. Many, impressed with the rapid growth of their plants, will want to use a pot that the plant will grow into. Nothing could be further from the needs of the plant. Always select the pot size appropriate to the root mass, not to the size of the leaves, or what you think the leaves will grow to by next year. This practice will allow you to water more frequently, which the plants will enjoy, while avoiding the danger of the buildup of sour, overwet spots in the medium. Both the growing medium selected and the environment dictate watering practices.

One of the changes in the mass culture of phals that has resulted in the most rapid increases in growth rates has been the use of media based on finer, more water retentive substances such as peat and coir, a coconut

Left: *Phal.* Amy Hausermann "Roman Holiday," while not up to modern standards for shape, is still prized for its intense color. (AM/AOS)

Above: *Phal. Maraldee* "Soroa Brilliance" is a brilliant modern yellow hybrid. (AM/AOS)

palm product. In the past, and to this day in more traditional nurseries and collections, growers selected coarser, faster-draining media such as fir bark or treefern. *Phalaenopsis* naturally grow faster than many orchids and are more prone to fungal and bacterial infections that affect their softer foliage. This explains why older European and English collections used handing baskets. It might also explain the continued use of coarse media today.

However, as growers began to look forward to maximize the growth of phals, they changed the media to be closer to those that were already in use on their other crops. This also makes sense in that it enables all cultural practices to be uniform throughout a facility. To their surprise (or perhaps not, as so many had little or no experience with orchids) they found that phals grown in a mix called "mud" by more experienced orchid growers gave extraordinary results. Watering is trickier in such media, but can be mastered. Salts will build up more critically, and, if allowed to overdry, the mix can be tough to rewet.

When purchasing plants grown in these finer media, be aware that the root system has developed in a constantly moist mix, in a humid greenhouse. Take this into account when putting the plant into your home. Do everything possible to reduce drought-induced stress to the plant. Many growers find that they are more comfortable with coarser media's greater tolerance for mistakes. If you think you might be, enjoy your new plants while in flower, but change over to your medium of preference in the spring immediately after flowering.

What is the most frequently asked question about orchids in general? "Where do I cut the spike?" Most orchids will flower once a year, the inflorescence ("flower spike") dies back and that is that. But many phals have the ability to branch from nodes (the little swollen areas on the flower stem) below the first flower. Somehow this has gained mythic powers with other orchids: "If I cut the spike, I'll lose something." Phals can give you more flowers from branches that arise from nodes below the first flower, so after the flower fades, simply cut between the last node and first flower scar. However, phals are also among the few orchids that will literally flower themselves to death. For this reason it is best to allow your plant only one branching per year. Removing the spike by May will allow the plant to grow strongly over the summer and produce another healthy spike in its normal winter season. Longer nights and cooler nights with a greater day-night temperature differential triggers the growth of flower spikes. If you'd like some of your plants to flower a bit sooner, and they've grown well by late summer, simply place them out-of-doors in a sheltered area or patio when temperatures drop into the low 60s or high 50s to trigger flower stems.

# VANDACEOUS

Giant, glistening saucer-shaped blooms in a rainbow of colors from earth tones through to reds, pinks, violets and blues, on into white, yellow and even green. A flowering *Vanda* plant, gleaming with moisture in the tropical sunlight, is a sight that few can forget. Such a scene evokes the tropics in a way matched by few other orchids. *Vandas* and their relatives are among the most tropical of all orchids. They revel in bright, hot sunshine, tempered with occasional heavy rains, that maintain the desired constantly high humidity. Unlike most all of the other orchids discussed in this book, vandaceous plants are monopodial (one-footed) as opposed to sympodial. In other words, they grow continuously from a single, often unbranching, growth point and may be erect or pendant.

Far Right: *V. Rothschildiana* "Blue Ribbon," a brilliant example of one of the most influential orchid hybrids of all time. (FCC/AOS)

Right: *Aerides crassifolia*, a fragrant species with pendant spikes.

Branching, where present, is often from the base or lower portions of the plant. While not a few of this group have terete, pencil-shaped leaves, most commonly seen *Vandas* outside of the tropics will have leaves that are strap-shaped to some extent. The flowering habit is generally upright, though some species have pendant spikes; while flowers vary from less than 1in to over 6in on the largest standard *Vanda* hybrids.

*Vandas* were among some of the earliest orchids described by Europeans, with the genus *Renanthera* dating from 1790 and the first *Vanda*, *roxburghii* (now synonymous with *tessellata*), in 1795. However, owing to their primarily tropical nature, they were not among the easiest of orchids for the European climate. Some of the higher-elevation species, such as *V. cristata* (first described in 1818), were more easily grown, though what should have been an equally easy species to cultivate, *V. coerulea* (described in 1837), retained the reputation of being difficult to grow right into the 20th century. Perhaps this can be laid at the

Left: *V. denisoniana* "Mary Motes" is very intolerant of cool temperatures. (FCC/AOS)

Below: *Ren. monachica* is a brightly colored *Vanda* relative often used in hybridizing for its color and rofusion of bloom.

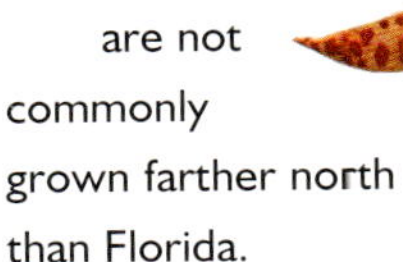

door of the practice of restricting the admission of sufficient fresh air, a holdover from the nineteenth-century days of the stoves. Between the description of *V. coerulea* and *V. sanderiana* (which some consider to be a different genus altogether, *Euanthe*) in 1882, ten more species were described, with only seven more to follow after *sanderiana*, for a total of around 30 species. Today, botanists may split out some of the terete-leafed *Vandas* into the separate genera of *Holcoglossum* and *Papilionanthe*. Owing to their need for higher light levels than can be comfortably provided in areas away from the Equator, these species are not commonly grown farther north than Florida.

Left: *Ascda.* Jannie Lee Brandt "Quick"—both plants show the cheery colors and profusion of bloom that make this type of hybrid so popular. (HCC/AOS)

If we were restricted to just these 30 or so species, (as we are in some other genera such as *Cymbidium*,) we would still have a nice hybrid complex, though only a relative few of the genus have contributed the lion's share of the genetics. Happily, we are not. The genus *Vanda* is just one part of the *Sarcanthinae*, horticulturally significant group of genera comprised of (to name just a few) *Renanthera*, *Aerides*, *Rhyncostylis*, *Ascocentrum* and, more distantly, *Neofinetia*. Within this group of genera, plant habit ranges from some of the tallest to some of the shortest; while flowers may be purest white to deepest wine. Most flowers are

Above: *Ascda* Su Fun Beauty "Mem. Jane Figiel". (AM/AOS)

small to intermediate in size, but make up for this in brilliance of color and profusion of bloom. Breeding with the very tropical genus *Arachnis* has given a race of hybrids ideally suited to cut-flower production in southeast Asia, though their need for high heat and sun makes them less satisfactory in more temperate zones, hence these plants are less often seen than are their cut-flower sprays.

However, we are primarily concerned with plants suited for their decorative use as potted plants, and that must be able to be cultivated reasonably well outside of the hottest tropics. Though most of this group do indeed require more heat and light and space than do many other orchids, there are those, too, that grow compactly, producing bright floral displays in conditions easily duplicated in many homes.

As with so many orchids, the only trick to success with these plants is interpreting their background in terms of proper care. Generally, the lower in elevation and closer to the Equator the species—or species

Right: *Asctm. miniatum* is a Thai species under-utilized in hybridizing, but very popular just as it is!

progenitors—grow, the less likely the plant is to grow and flower well away from those conditions. While growers in more northerly areas do succeed with vandaceous hybrids, it is not without the cost of additional care and, especially, heat.

## The species

Today, thanks to selective breeding of high quality parental stock, an excellent orchid collection can be based almost entirely on members of this group. Great public demand, coupled with more stringent regulations on wild-collected stock, has resulted in southeast Asian breeders producing exceptionally fine examples of the typical color varieties, as well as of unusual variations. In some cases, particularly in the most widely cultivated species, polyploidy mutations have worked their magic in producing yet still finer and more brightly colored examples. Three of the best known are *V. sanderiana*, *V. coerulea* and

Left: *Aer. lawrenceae* has an intricately formed lip that hides the column. It is highly perfumed.

*Asco. curvifolium*, which all have famous tetraploid strains. Of course, this supposed improvement over nature spurs debate over whether such highly inbred and manipulated plants can still be considered true species. In at least some cases, plants masquerading as species have proven to be not, rather highly inbred plants with hybrid origin. Nevertheless, there has never been a better time for amateurs to accumulate fine varieties of beautiful species, without having to raid the jungles to do so. Because the main contributing genera can all be discussed within the confines of this text, each genus will be briefly described in alphabetic order.

### *Aerides*

Upright to pendulous plants with broad, overlapping strap leaves, and pendant inflorescenses, *Aerides* are known for their slightly bizarre lips and extravagant perfume. Most often found in shades of lilac, lavender and white, the smallish blooms cascade freely from the most recently matured leaf-axils. *Aerides* easily make huge plants, especially when naturalized in frost-free gardens, and such plants give a profusion of bloom second to none. Early in the history of orchid growing, large specimens were imported and as such caused much exc ted comment at horticultural expositions.

Some of the most commonly seen species in this group are *Aer. houlettiana*, *Aer. crassifolia* and *Aer. fieldingii* (syn. *rosea*). *Aerides* prefer, (or at least will tolerate), slightly more shade than will many of the other members of this group, making them ideal for higher-latitude areas.

The last ten years or so has also seen an explosion in the popularity of this genus in hybridizing with other members of the Sarcanthinae.

### *Ascocentrum*

This small genus contains some of the most attractive of all orchid species, one of which has been vitally important in the development of a major horticultural type. *Asctm. curvifolium*, the species most important to hybridizing, looks much like a small *Vanda* plant, with strap leafs and an upright stem. Brightest red-orange, smallish

blooms are borne on straight, tall spikes. Most modern *Ascocendas* (*Ascocentrum* x *Vanda*) contain this species. The two other most popular species in this genus are smaller than *curvifolium* and have thicker, shorter leaves closely held on compact plants. *Asctm. miniatum* and *Asctm. ampullaceum* have yellow orange and rose blooms, respectively, though *miniatum*'s spikes emerge more cleanly from the foliage. *Asctm. miniatum* and *ampullaceum* have contributed to the breeding of novelty types that will be discussed later.

Plants in this genus will also flower relatively well with slightly less light than is normally required for *Vandas*, and it is easier to get light to the plants owing to their diminutive size. Here, we see a variety of unusual color forms entering cultivation as a result of select breeding, with *Asctm. curvifolium*

Left: *Rhy. retusa* Alba is a white form of this beautiful foxtail orchid.

*aurea* (yellow), and *Asctm. ampullaceum* in white or pink forms. There is, additionally, some debate as to the exact identity of what has been known in collections for so long as *miniatum*. Some taxonomists give one name, some another. For now, it is safest to remain with *miniatum*.

## *Neofinetia*

This is a monotypic (one species, *falcata*, only) genus native to Japan, where it is revered as one of the classic orchid species. Petite plants give short spikes of highly perfumed bird-like white blooms. A large specimen plant will often fit into no more than a 4in pot. *Neofinetia falcata* is important as much for its intrinsic beauty as for its role as the progenitor of a new type of potted plant orchid hybrid. *Neofinetia* and its hybrids will often tolerate much more coolness than will others of this type.

## *Renanthera*

Most of this genus are taller than can be comfortably contained in most temperate collections, but several—notably *monachica* and *imschootiana*—are fairly commonly grown. *Renantheras* are widely cultivated in tropical areas as cut-flowers, and even as decorative hedging, where their profusion of highly colored blooms splash the landscape with red and scarlet during much of the year. However, growers in less tropical zones will sometimes commit the space and heat necessary to do well with larger species or hybrids

Right: *Ascda.* Princes Mikasa "Blue Angel" is one of the most prolific bloomers in this section, often blooming several or more times per year. (HCC/AOS)

of *Renanthera*, and spring orchid shows come alive with the arrow-head shaped branching infloresenses. The brilliance of color given by *Renanthera* species makes them important parents.

### *Rhyncostylis*

The three popular species in this genus—*gigantea*, *coelestis* and *retusa*—are all moderately sized plants that are well-known members of many orchid collections. Two of them, *gigantea* and *coelestis*, also represent a good case study of the value of line breeding. Known best as foxtail orchids owing to their upright to arching inflorescences of smallish blooms, rhyncostylis can be among the most decorative of monopodials in their various seasons. *Rhyn. coelestis* is a special favorite that comes in several color forms, as does *Rhyn. gigantea*, including white, spotted and nearly pure wine red. Plants are not too big, maturing nicely in a 6-8in basket, with *coelestis* branching freely from the base to form a nice clump quite quickly. Each of these two species has a special role in modern vandaceous breeding.

### *Vanda*

While this genus has a reputation for large plants, only a relative few of the species grow too large for temperate collections. This includes such species as *V. sanderiana*, *V. tricolor* and *V. luzonica*, all of which, unfortunately, have played a major role in the development of our modern hybrid types and can easily reach 3-4ft plus in height. Even the blue *V. coerulea* is not an unreasonably large plant, though it can easily get to 30in or so. There are several other species with great horticultural importance such as *V. tessellata*, as well as *V. deari* and *V. denisoniana*, both of which have made vital contributions to the breeding of yellow *Vanda* hybrids.

With 25 or so other species, it is just not practical to mention all by name, although those inclined to such things will find a rich literature available to them. The *Vandas* that do not grow in tropical climates are the exception rather than the rule, and these include two of the earliest to be discovered, *V. cristata* and *V. coerulea*, both of which come from higher elevations and will not tolerate too much warmth. Another attractive higher-elevation species is *V. coerulescens*.

## The hybrids

*Vanda* and related hybrids make up a multi-million dollar per year market for southeast Asian growers. Especially in the last ten years, great advances in the quality of standard types, as well as in the proliferation of novelty potted plant varieties have resulted in a hybrid complex of rich complexity and extreme diversity. Plant size and flower size, flower count, frequency of bloom and rapidity of growth have all been profoundly influenced by the revolution in the potted plant industry. Where the traditional round "saucer" *Vandas* remain vital in this changing market, especially in the more specialized hobby trade, their relatively slow growth, more seasonal

Right: *Rhy. coelestis* is playing an important role in the production of modern potted plant types.

Right: *V. coerulescens*

flowering and large plant size, make them less attractive to the potted plant grower who must look at turnover per bench square foot as his prime meridian. Breeding with faster growing, smaller, freer-blooming and less heat-demanding species has given us a whole new horticultural type to enjoy.

*Vanda* breeding has not always been so popular. Indeed, the only *Vanda* hybrid registered in the 19th century was from a naturally pollinated plant, *V.* Miss Joaquim (*teres x hookeriana*, neither considered true *Vandas* today), although this plant can fairly be said to have started the southeast Asian cut-flower trade by its free-flowering traits. The first two hybrids in this group to utilize strap-leaf parents were registered in 1919, both using *V. tricolor*, *V.* Gilbert Triboulet (x *coerulea*) and *V.* Tatzeri ( x *sanderiana*).

The most logical hybrid, with the most popular and obvious parents was not even registered until 1931, *V.* Rothschildiana (*sanderiana x coerulea*). With this happy marriage, the modern standard was set. Both parents, while each lovely in its own right, had drawbacks. *V. sanderiana* was slow growing and large, needed lots of warmth, had rather dull-colored, earth-toned blooms, with relatively narrow petals and a bunchy spike habit. *V. coerulea* grew well enough, and had a lovely blue tessellation, but the petals tended to twist around almost back on themselves. Today, seeing as we do the products of generations of species in breeding, it is hard to remember such drawbacks.

Growing interest in the Hawaiian islands in the 1940s and 1950s led to increasingly fine progeny from these two basic species, augmented with *tricolor*, *luzonica*, and *deari*, to give brighter and more varied colors. *V. tricolor* and *V. luzonica* genes gave vibrant reds, pinks, and purples, while *V. deari* has contributed much (later along with *V. denisoniana*) to modern yellows. In the 1960s, breeders in Singapore and Malaysia stole the march from the Hawaiians, though the standards of excellence established by these pioneers remained. What we know today as modern standard *Vandas* are the result of the efforts of Thai breeders since the 1970s, based on their ability to grow and flower so many plants, which enabled them to select highly superior breeding stock.

Modern ascocendas got their start with the use of *Asctm. curvifolium* to produce both *Ascda.* Meda Arnold and Yip Sum Wah, which, to this day, still have a place in breeding programs. *Ascda.* Yip Sum Wah, though registered over 40 years ago, remains one of the most highly awarded orchids of all time. Moderately sized plants often give multiple flowerings over the year, and require somewhat less heat and light to perform well than do most *Vandas*. Additionally, these plants flower younger than do *Vandas*. In today's ascocendas, we can see the multiple fine traits of full-size *Vandas*, including the extraordinary color array, in a much more compact package.

Brilliance of color and a more compact, freer-flowering nature is behind much of the most forward-thinking breeding, giving rise to hybrids like *Ascda.* Princess Mikasa and *Ascda.* Su Fun Beauty that, in addition to their undeniable beauty, seem almost never to be out of bloom.

More complex, intergeneric hybrids are also seen more and more. *Renanthera* is used for rich red color and branching spike habit to give *Kagawaras* (*Asctm.* x *V.* x *Ren.*). *Aerides* give *Christiearas* (*Aer.* x *Asctm.* x *V.*), known for their soft colors and beautiful spikes of heavy-substanced blooms. However, it is with *Rhyncostylis* that we are seeing the widest array of great advances, both in standard types, as well as in novelties. *Rhyn. gigantea* is used to breed exceptionally dark, wine-colored *Rhyncovandas*, while *Rhyn. coelestis* has more importantly given us *Vascostylis* (*Asctm.* x *Rhyn.* x *V.*). These often make for improved *ascocendas*, with a broad range of colors and foxtail-like spikes that give a spectacular display.

Lastly, an entire group of new potted-plant subjects has arisen from the use of *Neofinetia falcata*. Whether with *Vandas*, *Ascocendas*, *Ascocentrums*, or *Rhyncostylis*, *Neofinetia* gives a distinct charm and fragrance to its hybrids that make them much in demand. *Neostylis* Lou Sneary (*Neo. falcata* x *Rhyn. coelestis*) is one of the best examples of this type. Additionally, great advances in the basic species building-blocks have led to successful remakes of many other hybrids of all of the above-named. Lastly, breeders have so successfully searched out the best-growing plants with which to breed that we have plants that are far superior in growth habit than have ever been available during any era.

## The care

With a few very notable exceptions, *Vandas* and their related hybrids are best grown in a greenhouse or out-of-doors in frost-free sub-tropical gardens and patios. By and large, the plants are too big, too demanding of high light and humidity, and require watering too frequently to be practical under home conditions. The best vandaceous plants are grown in slatted wooden

Right: *Rhv.* Bangkok Sky Happy Summer has unique coloration influenced by an alba parent. (AM/AOS)

baskets with little or no media—depending on grower preference and climatic need—with high light, heat, and humidity. Such treatment will allow the large, rambling roots to roam freely in and around the baskets' slats, as well as hang freely in the air, where they can more easily absorb the frequent applications of water and fertilizer they crave.

A good root system is needed to support the monopodial growth habit with its paucity of water-storage, and allow the best growth with subsequent flower production. Since many of these plants will do best with nearly full sun, except at noonday, it is imperative that sufficient humidity and watering be provided, as well as the requisite fertilizer. Watering should be copious, running freely through the basket and around the roots, until their green color shows that they have been thoroughly wetted. Only in the driest areas should any medium be used in the pots, as this will tend to interfere with the preferred, rapid wet-dry cycle and will also necessitate more frequent repotting. *Vandas* and their relatives should have their roots disturbed as infrequently as practical, to avoid the inevitable damage and setback that occurs. Attempt such disturbance only when fresh root activity is evident, as in the spring and summer months.

The exceptions to the above cultural rules are those plants that are sufficiently dwarfed—such as *Ascocentrums* and some *Ascocendas* bred from *Asctm. miniatum*—to allow their needs to be more reasonably accommodated in the home. Also, those bred from more temperature-tolerant backgrounds, such as *Neo. falcata* and its hybrids may be grown in the home with other high light orchids, providing that adequate humidity and watering is provided. Any of this type of hybrid or species are wonderful home decorative subjects when conditions allow and may be worth the extra effort required to do well.

Right: *V. coerulea*

# OTHER INTERESTING ORCHIDS

## All the (many) others

After all that has been said about the vastness and intrigue of the orchid family, how strange to think that it could possibly be contained between two covers, in eight or nine chapters. Yet that has been the intent, to give a general overview of the tale of orchids, an introduction. So much has been left unsaid. The next few pages will go beyond the more commonly seen plants that have been the subject until this point, in an attempt to illustrate the diversity contained in other groups. Groups less commonly seen outside of specialist circles, certainly, but still representative of plants with enough appeal and beauty to warrant mention.

This chapter will deal with groups known as tribes, rather than individual genera—though representative genera belonging to each tribe under discussion will be enumerated—so that more ground may be covered in the limited available space. With such a wide variety of orchids to cover, cultural needs will vary all over the world. Some will be among the best and most popular houseplants, others will need a greenhouse, while others still will make good subjects for naturalizing in the subtropical garden where frost does not threaten.

Taxonomy, the science of placing organisms into an ordered system, is intended to show evolutionary, not spatial or physical, relationships. When particular organisms are grouped by other criteria than having

Above: *Pleurothallis truncata* is just one of the many bizarre members of this extensive tribe.

Right: *Coel. pandurata* "Bessey Creek," an Old World species often known as the "black orchid" for the markings on its lip . (HCC/AOS)

descended from common ancestors—for example, by their physical appearance or by the fact that they may grow together—the system is known as artificial. Most of the groups, or tribes, that we will be covering will be related by common ancestry and known as natural, or "monophyletic." Some, though, will simply be a matter of convenience. It is simply easier to group certain genera together. While they may all be loosely and distantly related, it may also be because none of them really fit anywhere else in this book. Natural tribes will be listed under the name of the best-known or common genus.

## "Old World"

*Coelogyne* is a rather diverse genus ranging from moderate elevations in the Indian Himalayas to tropical Southeast Asia and the Pacific rim islands. Obviously, these plants inhabit

Left: *Dendrochilum cobbianum*.

Right: *Bulbophyllum phalaenopsis*.

a variety of ecological niches. Some, like *Coel. pandurata* and *speciosa*, come from lower elevations and need to be grown in a greenhouse where they can be protected from cool temperatures. *Pandurata* grows rather large because of the distance between pseudobulbs and needs a lot of room to do well.

On the other hand, the groups of species from the higher elevations need cooler temperatures to do their best. Species like the crystal white, fragrant, *Coel. cristata* and *ochracea* do best under *Cymbidium* conditions, if given more shade. Another white *Coelogyne* that must be among the most beautiful of all orchids is *Mooreana*, recently rediscovered in Vietnam. The flowers are large for the genus, pure white and very shapely. One trait shared by all members of this genus is their

Left: *Zootrophion hirtzii* is a member of the *Pleurothallid* group that opens only slightly to admit a very small pollinator.

Above: *Angraecum leonis*.

habit of flowering from the developing new growths. All intensely resent the disturbance of repotting, as well, so potting should be infrequent and carefully done.

*Dendrochilum* is a rapidly evolving and speciating genus centered in Borneo. Commonly known as the "Chain" or "Rattlesnake" orchids for their flowering habit, *Dendrochilums* are coming to be more appreciated in specialist circles. *Dendrochilums* get their name from the prominent, imbricate bracts that subtend each rather insignificant flower, giving the appearance of a chain. Some of the most often seen are *Dend. cobbianum, magnum,* and *filiforme*, a particularly nicely flowered form. *Dend. magnum* is a wonderful display plant, perhaps the largest of the genus, with a musky perfume. Its cascades of cream-bracted burnt orange blooms are a sight to behold in their late fall season.

*Dendrochilums* seem to be generally easy to grow under *Cattleya* conditions if given slightly more shade and moisture. Plants do best if left to grow into multiple growth specimens, where the multitude of spikes will be quite impressive.

It is a pity to have to consign such a numerous and diverse genus as *Bulbophyllum* to the "back of the book." One of the largest genera, with over 1,000 species, perhaps no other group of orchids is growing faster in popularity among serious orchid enthusiasts. Taxonomists have created several smaller genera from *Bulbophyllum*, including *Cirrhopetalum* and *Megaclinium*. "Bulbos" have few characteristics that would instantly link them in the inexperienced eye, yet have enough general similarities so that it is fairly easy to discern

one even if it is impossible to know all the species. Some of the very smallest of all orchids are *Bulbophyllums*. *B. globuliforme*, *B. minutissimum*, and *B. odoardii* all are less than a quarter of an inch in height. Yet, some of the largest, if not strangest, are also bulbos, such as *B. phalaenopsis* with leaves that can reach well over three foot and flowers that smell like rotting meat. This is not uncommon in *Bulbophyllum*, many of whose members are pollinated by flies.

*Bulbophyllum* can also lay claim to some of the largest flowers in the family, with the recently rediscovered *B. echinolabium* as a front-runner in this claim. It is impossible to generalize; though many of this genus have a good distance between pseudobulbs, giving them a rambling habit best contained in a basket or on a mount. Some are good in pots, too. As these are largely grown on mounts or in baskets, their need for humidity puts them beyond the reach of the typical home grower.

Left: *Masd. angulifera* is one of the smaller-flowered of the group.

Some of the *Cirrhopetalums*, the "Daisy" orchids, grow compactly, or at least are small enough to be candidates for the dedicated windowsill hobbyist. *Cattleya* temperatures, *Phalaenopsis* light, and adequate humidity seem to be required. Some growers claim that the constant moisture regime of sitting in a pan of water is of benefit, though these growers tend to take more time with their plants than most of us can afford.

Above: *Masd. hirtzii* is a warmer-growing member of a usually cool-growing genus.

### *Angraecoids*

Centered in Africa, spreading to Madagascar and the Mascarene Islands, this group of genera is largely moth-pollinated, as demonstrated by their night-fragrant, ghostly white or pale green blooms with long nectar-bearing spurs. Indeed, it is based on one of these, *Angraecum sesquipedale*, that Charles Darwin made his prediction of the existence of a moth, not yet discovered, with the 18 inch proboscis necessary to get to the base of the equally long nectary. It was ultimately found and named *Xanthopan morganii praedicta*.

*Angraecum, Jumiellias, Aeranthes, Aerangis, Amesiella,* and other, smaller genera make up this group of monopodial orchids. Some, such as *Ang. eburneum*, are large plants requiring lots of space; while others, such as *Aerangis rhodosticta* or *Amesiella philippenensis*, are miniatures hardly taking up any space at all. As might be expected, most grow in rather warm and humid environments where their lack of water-storage capacity will not be a problem. However, some *Aerangis* grow in areas with

seasonally dry periods that can last seven or more months. Generally, though, these plants will grow well with *Cattleyas* or *Phalaenopsis*, depending on their origin. Some will make nice garden or patio specimens where frost does not threaten, and their large size is more easily accommodated.

## *Pleurothallids*

A 1999 demographic survey by the American Orchid Society showed that both paphs and *Pleurothallids* came in last in the "most preferred" category, with only approximately 34 percent of those responding giving such a rating. Yet, like paphs, *Pleurothallids* (as they are known) do inspire fanatic devotion among their adherents.

*Pleurothallids*, as a New World group, have many ecological and pollinator similarities with the equally large and diverse Old World genus (or group, if you prefer) *Bulbophyllum*. The familiar image of the

Left: *Masd. ignea* "Fluorescent" is a cool-growing, high-altitude species.

Above: *Stan. impressa* is another rare conjunction of a ephemeral bloom and a judging session.

lonely orchid, barely hanging on in a changing environment is a popular one; but there are many, many other orchids that are adapting and radiating freely, with speciation at a fever pitch. *Pleurothallids* are one such grouping. This has led to the diversity and great range of habitat occupied by these plants. Most, though, occupy higher elevations where cool temperatures and high humidity are the rule.

Where *Pleurothallids* are plentiful, they are plentiful indeed. Trees may seem to be literally covered with a variety of species, many of which seem to form almost moss-like carpeting over the branches. For example, along the famous Inca Trail leading to and from Macchu Picchu, *Pleurothallid* genera are locally abundant, that is, almost weed-like in their ubiquity. The selective buyer may find both species and hybrids from lower elevation plants that will be more adaptable, but most grow on the cool side.

The overall diminutive stature and tendency to flower on and off throughout the year have made *Pleurothallids* the "darling" of the underlights and windowsill growers, as well as highly popular in more northern climes such as the northeast and Pacific northwest. Where the environment either matches that preferred by genera like *Pleurothallis, Masdevallia, Trisetella, Zootrophion, Dresslerella, Resptrepia,* and others, or can be controlled to do so, growers can expect fast-growing and free-flowering plants with an overall attractive look that is hard to match. This particular aspect of *Pleurothallids* is the one that keeps the cognoscenti coming back for more: a well-grown and flowered plant of just about anything in this group is among the prettiest, most fascinating of all orchids.

The foliage is often handsome, consisting of upright bladed leaves growing in clumps. The flowers may be of brilliant or muted colors and odd shapes, impossibly small or disproportionately large, well above the leaves on upright stems or hanging beneath the plant on strictly pendant inflorescences, single or many. Diversity is the rule, not the exception.

Where their needs can be met, *Pleurothallids* are also among the fastest-growing, earliest-flowering subjects for hybridizing. Breeders are especially fond of *Masdevallia*, where they are creating an entirely new horticultural type of brightly colored and free-blooming potted plants that make superb displays in the smallest pots, often just three–four inches. A fused sepalline tube is what makes the show on a *Masdevallia*, with the lip and petals often out of view and insignificant. The aspect is often of stylized kites fluttering above the plant, in colors of white to orange, yellow and red, often spotted with contrasting colors. Both cool and warmer growing parents are in use, so make sure to consult the vendor before committing to a purchase.

Above: *Lyc.* Andy Easton "Geyserland" and Stan. impressa "Crownfox," (AM/AOS)

In general, *Pleurothallids* prefer to be underpotted—which isn't easy, considering how small many of the plants really are—in a fine, well-drained medium that will retain some moisture. The fine roots will benefit from a mix that can be freely watered often, while not breaking down or staying too wet. Most *Pleurothallids* also grow best under fairly shady conditions, as for phals or paphs, where high light will not cause

unacceptable heat build-up in the tender leaves. Fertilizing should be at no more than one-quarter label strength, at weekly intervals, interspersing monthly leachings with clean water. These orchids won't tolerate salt, so good, clean water of the highest quality is imperative as in nature they are used to high rainfall and evenly moist conditions. Good observational habits are a must, and go hand-in-hand with sanitation.

Because *Pleurothallids* are such small, tender plants, sucking pests such as mealybugs, aphids, and scale can very quickly kill an infested favorite if not treated in a timely fashion. Also, aphids are known to transmit viruses between plants in this group, and entire collections have succumbed before the grower was even aware there was a problem.

### *Catasetum/Cycnoches/Mormodes*

If one were searching for the right word to describe this and the following, distantly related group, it might be "otherworldly." This tribe, technically known as the *Catasetiinae*, is for the most part deciduous, flowering from pseudobulbs matured during the summer growing season. If the flowering season is more toward fall, the leaves may still be on the plant, while those that do not flower until later in the winter will probably have dropped their leaves. *Catasetum*-types have medium size, cigar-shaped pseudobulbs with broad, soft, plicate leaves at intervals up the height of the bulb. Flower spikes may be borne in the leaf axils near the top of the bulb as in *Mormodes* or *Cycnoches*, or nearer the bottom as in *Catasetum*. In nature, *Catasetinae* are a type of orchid that tends to colonize disturbed habitats rather quickly and be of a temporary nature. For example, it is not uncommon to see *Catasetums* or *Mormodes* on rotting stumps or on fenceposts.

A variety of unusual and distinctive features set this group apart, and more than make up for the rather ephemeral nature of the blooms, which, at best, will only last a week or two. *Catasetums*, and the closely related *Clowesia*, have medium-length, pendant spikes of often bird-like blooms in

Left: *Coryanthes gernotii* "JEM," is related to Stanhopeas, and is known as the "Bucket Orchid" for its bizarre lip structure designed to capture bees and thereby ensure pollination. (CBR/AOS)

exotic colorations. There has been some hybridization done with *Catasetums* that has resulted in some of the very darkest of all orchid flowers. *Catasetum tenebrosum* is deep, rich mahogany, while *Catasetum* Susan Fuchs has rich, burgundy markings.

*Cycnoches*, also known as Swan Orchids, have very long, pendant inflorescences of bizarre and intricate blooms. *Catasetum* have pollinia that eject themselves at the pollinating vector with some degree of force. This can be quite a shock to someone getting too close with his or her nose! Lastly, *Catasetum* and *Cycnoches* also share the unusual habit of having unisexual flowers. That is, they have two sorts of flowers, often not borne at the same time on the same plant, one female and one male. The male flowers often appear in greater numbers and are the horticulturally desirable (showy) form of the flower. Female flowers tend to be fewer in number and resemble each other between species. *Mormodes* generally have upright to slightly arching spikes, whose blooms have petals and sepals swept back from the forward-thrust lip and column. The lip is often twisted around the column. Hybrids within this group have produced some of the first truly "black" orchids.

## The care

Culture for this group is slightly specialized, owing to their very seasonal growth cycle. *Cattleya* conditions, with bright light, moderate humidity, and temperatures, suit well the year around. However, after the season's growth is matured, (usually by late summer or early fall,) watering and fertilizing should stop. Do not water during the resting period so as to allow the leaves to naturally fall. Some growers even completely remove the plants from their pots just in case they might forget and inadvertently water at the wrong time. Repotting is best done as new growth and rooting initiates in the fall.

Many orchids of this type need to be kept divided down to no more than the lead bulb and emerging growth, with backbulbs used for propagation. If more backbulbs are left in the division, they

Right: *Cstm. tenebrosum* is an orchid species that can truly approach black coloration.

will simply wither as the front portion grows, while if they are severed, they will give a new plant. Whatever medium is used should drain well, but retain good moisture. Watering during growth should be frequent and accompanied by copious fertilizer, especially as the root system fills the pot. All this gives the plant maximum opportunity to make up the optimal growth for the season, so that flowering will be heavy. The only pest problem that these plants, and others with large soft leaves, may face is spider mite. Spider mite can be kept down by maintaining good humidity, periodically washing the leaves down top and bottom, and keeping a good eye out for the symptoms of silvering and "weeping" of the undersides of the leaves.

### Stanhopeas

*Catasetinae* have bizarre, medium-size blooms that last a moderate time. *Stanhopeas* and their relatives—*Embreea, Acineta, Lueddemanniana, Paphinia, Gongora, Coryanthes,* and a few others—have generally large, highly-perfumed blooms that last only a day or two in full perfection. To add to the esoteric nature of these plants, inflorescences emerge straight down from the lead pseudobulbs, so plants must be grown in baskets that allow the growing spike to escape and flower. Such a strategy puts a great deal of energy into a short flowering

Left: *Ctsm.* Susan Fuchs "Burgundy Chips,"—it is seldom that one of these short-lived blooms is in synch with a local judging session; rarer yet when it is deemed worthy of the highest award. (FCC/AOS)

Above: *Gongora quinquenervis* is in the *Stanhopiinae*, with pendant spikes of bird-like blooms.

event, while that of the *Catasetiinae* (and others) is designed to keep the flowers available to potential pollinating vectors for a longer period of time.

The *Stanhopea* tribe is known as the *Stanhopiinae*, and is a group strictly for specialists, owing to their often large size and short-lived blooms. Someone accustomed to *Phals* or *Paphs* just won't be satisfied with flowers that they might miss if not at home on just the right day. And this is exactly what happens: the inflorescence, with a few or dozens of buds, grows rather quickly, buds swell and swell far beyond what seems to be reasonable, until finally one morning the flowers burst open with an audible "pop," filling the growing area with their aroma. After a day—or two at most—the flowers fade quickly and fold, leaving only a memory. *Stanhopea*, the closely related *Embreea, Paphinia* and *Coryanthes*, tend to have inflorescences with one or two to as many as eight or ten blooms. *Acineta* and *Lueddemanniana*, on the other hand, have a wealth of flowers along their long, pendant inflorescences,

Left: *Gongora maculata*.

Above: *Masd. lehmanii* is a multifloral species in this Pleurothallid genus. It is highly perfumed, unlike most other members of the genus.

with *Acineta* blooms a little larger than *Lueddemanniana*, which compensates with more blooms. While *Stanhopeas* take up a lot of space, they are not otherwise difficult to cultivate, growing happily under *Cattleya* conditions, if given a bit more shade and moisture. The large leaves can be suscepti-ble to salt damage, so care must be taken in proper watering and fertilizing, with an eye toward keeping the mix evenly moist. Frequent, light fertilizing is called for. As with *Catasetiinae*, spider mites can be a problem if not monitored, or if humidity is allowed to fall too low. However, *Stanhopeas* are not deciduous and therefore should not be given a totally dry rest, though if growth slows, and the medium is drying slowly, it might be wise to reduce watering. The main thing to remember about this group is that they must be grown in slatted or wire baskets, or on mounts (if humidity and watering needs can be accommodated,) to allow the spikes

Above: *Masd. macrura*—one of the most popular groups for windowsill and underlights growers is the *Pleurothallid* group. This series of photos shows why, with the vast range of color and form, folks never seem to tire of these sometimes demanding plants.

Above: *Masd. coccinea*.

to grow down through the medium and flower.

### *Zygopetalum*

As with the *Pleurothallids*, there is much contemporary interest in this group of genera, popularly known as "soft leafed" and technically as the *Zygopetaliinae*. Plants may or may not have discernible pseudobulbs, though all have the stem base—and pseudobulb, if present—sheathed by the bases of the large, soft leaves. Many of this group have fan-shaped growth with an elongate rhizome that grows upward, resulting in a climbing habit. Plant size will vary from truly miniature as in *Promenaea*,

Above: *Drac. vampira.*

Above: *Masd. norops.*

*Colax*, and some *Cochleanthes*, to the more moderately sized *Huntleya, Galeottia*, and *Zygopetalum* itself.

The only plants that present difficulties are those with rambling rhizomes that will quickly grow out of a container. Some of these, such as *Huntleya meleagris* and *Zygo. maxillare*, can be grown on tree fern totems or otherwise mounted. *Zygos* are not, in general, difficult plants to grow. Many do well on the cool and shady side of *Cattleya* conditions, preferring to be kept evenly moist. *Zygopetalums*, in particular, can be very forgiving of abuse and are often grown as garden companions to Cymbidiums in frost-free areas of the West Coast.

It is in the *Zygos* where we find some of the colors closest to blue in the orchid family, with some members of *Zygopetalum*

Above: *Psnth.* Star Sapphire "Star of Miami," illustrates new inroads in the breeding in the *Zygopetalum* group, with unusual color results. (HCC/AOS)

having intensely blue-veined lips and the *Pescatorea* species with an overall blue-violet color. *Acacallis cyanea* is famous as a "blue" orchid, as is *Cochleanthes* discolor with its blue lip and "Vaporub" perfume. Indeed, breeders have done quite a bit of work with *Zygos* to produce the most intensely blue orchids possible.

Above: *Huntleya meleagris* shows bronzy flowers from fan-shaped growths.

Combinations of *Acacallis* with *Colax* (*Aclx.* "Eva's Blue Amazon") and *Pescatorea* with *Cochleanthes* (*Psnth.* "Star Sapphire") give evidence of the breeder's intent, if only with their names and not with the results.

*Zygopetalums* have long been popular with breeders, *Zygo*. B.G. White and Arthur Elle having the status of classic orchids, remaining in cultivation for decades. Modern work has been centered largely in New Zealand and Australia owing to the group's popularity as *Cymbidium* companions, though U.S. growers are attempting to make *Zygos* into standard potted plant subjects. The limited color palette, short season, and uncertainty as to flowering age would seem to make this a little risky, though. This entire group is known for exotic and pungent fragrance, one plant often being enough to perfume an entire room or growing area.

There are a few important generalizations that can be

Above: *Aclx.* Eva's Blue Amazon is an intergeneric hybrid in the *Zygopetalum* group.

Above: *Zygo.* Syd Monkhouse "Putu" shows the level of improvement in the breeding of this genus. (AM/AOS)

inferred from the growth habit of each species or hybrid. The smaller the plant, the finer and more moisture-retentive the medium needs to be. A similar rule of thumb holds true for presence or absence of pseudobulbs, where the larger the bulb, the less atmospheric moisture will be necessary for the plant's well being, and the more light it will enjoy.

The fan-shaped plants like *Huntleya* will need to be fairly shady and moist to do well. None of this group can be considered cool growing, though most are definitely moderate growers. They prefer temperatures on the cool side of *Cattleya* conditions with the least diurnal variation possible. Temperature swings are what stresses the constitution of these plants most.

## *Maxillaria*

*Maxillaria*, as a genus, is another of the largest and the most widespread of orchid types. It may seem a puzzle that some of the largest groups—such as *Pleurothallids, Maxillaria*, and *Bulbophyllum*—are put into the "back of the book." But, widespread and successful does not always translate necessarily into showy and popular. Just as in the other large genera, there are a good number of very beautiful and worthwhile members, but there are many more that do not merit attention in horticultural circles. However, perhaps no other genus, with the possible exception of *Dendrobium*, can boast the wide range of plant habits that *Maxillaria* can. From the tiniest little plants with miniscule and plainly colored flowers, through to enormous plants that have a "pseudomonopodial" habit and miniscule and plainly colored flowers,

Below: *Max. sopfhonitis* is a brightly colored, higher elevation member of this incredibly diverse genus.

Above: *Max. speciosa* shows yet another variation on a theme in *Maxillaria*. This photo was taken near the species' native habitat in Cali, Colombia.

*Maxillaria* has a reputation for inconsequential blooms that is only now being eclipsed. Indeed, for some, the name *Maxillaria* is synonymous with "packing material" as a lot of the time in the past, the *Maxillaria* species were used to cushion other, more important orchids. A lot of the time too, when a new grower would order a "selection of species, our choice" from an importer, it would be a selection of unnamed *Maxillaria* species.

It is nearly impossible to generalize about culture, as *Maxillarias* may grow from high-elevation cloud forest conditions with a saturated atmosphere, to dry sea-level scrub where the only moisture is nightly dew. As with the plants, flower-size ranges from under an inch to over ten inches or more in some of the larger-flowered species such as *Max. sanderiana* or *Max. speciosa*. Fragrance, too, differs greatly.

Above: *Bif. harrisoniae* is related to *Maxillaria* and *Lycaste*, and blooms from the base of the pseudobulbs.

*Max. tenuifolia* is one of the most beautifully perfumed orchids and is known as the coconut pie orchid as a result.

*Maxillaria*, as a group, known as the *Maxillariianae*, contains *Scuticaria, Lycaste, Bifrenaria,* and a few others. *Scuticaria* is one of the family's curiosities, with whip-like, pendant leaves that may reach four foot or more. The flowers are leopard spotted and arise near the rhizome. These are clearly best grown on mounts. *Bifrenaria* is a moderately-sized genus and contains some popular species such as *Bif. harrisoniae*. These prove difficult for some to flower, though *Bifrenaria* has been used to make bigeneric hybrids with *Lycaste* to make the even more difficult-to-flower *Lycasteria*.

It is in *Lycaste* that this group has attained its greatest appeal. Hybrids from *Lyc. skinneri*—itself a beautiful orchid and the national flower of Guatemala—have

reached a pinnacle of perfection that is almost difficult to imagine, in a range of colors from nearly orange to pastel pink and white, and on to reds. Large plants, with broad plicate leaves, *Lyc. skinneri* types are not for everyone, if only because the plants are difficult to accommodate. Even larger are the intergeneric hybrids with the related genus *Anguloa*, where pseudobulbs reach prodigious size, the size ameliorated by the production of copious blooms from the base of each new growth. *Anguloa* and *Lycaste* both flower from the base of the developing new growth, with each inflorescence bearing one flower, though there may be twenty or more produced from each growth.

The more easily cultivated *Lycastes* are from the Mexican and Central American deciduous group, which have seasonal growth and drop their leaves before flowering in spring. The most popular in this group is *Lyc. aromatica*, loved for its beautiful cinnamon scent and floriferous habit. The characteristic flower shape of *Lycastes*, as well as many *Maxillarias*, is triangular, with the sepals forming the dominant feature of the flower, the petals and lip held closely to the column and less prominent.

The large, soft leaves of *Lycastes* demand lots of water both while growing, as well as when at their full development. They are also susceptible to water damage, as well as marring by physical damage and by improper pesticide use. Generally, *Lyc. skinneri*, its hybrids, and relatives, prefer to be evenly moist all year round, with a slight

Left: *Phaius tankervillae* is a popular garden plant where frost does not threaten.

Above: *Bletilla striata*.

drying in winter as the water needs decrease naturally. On the other hand, the deciduous *Lycastes, Aromatica, Deppei, Consobrina,* and others, will want to have a pronounced dry rest in the winter to spur flowering.

## Terrestrials

Terrestrial orchids have been mildly popular over the years, but recently have been at the heart of a new trend with new and old varieties being propagated for wider usage. The terrestrial orchids that are most popular now fall easily into two categories: those grown for their flowers and those grown for their foliage.

Above: *Calanthe vestita*.

Foliage orchids have been around for years, of course, and most are known as "jewel orchids." These plants, usually *Haemaria (Ludisia)* discolor, are grown for their beautiful burgundy wine-colored leaves strikingly marked with red lines. There are a variety of closely related genera, with one of the best known in the U.S. being one of our natives, *Goodyera pubescens*, with its light green leaves and white netting. Any or all of these may be grown as terrarium plants or as potted specimens. In some cases, greenhouse growers like to use these plants under their benches as a sort of groundcover.

As the popularity of this type grows, more and more obscure species are being introduced to specialist growers at orchid shows and similar venues. Jewel orchids are denizens of the shady forest floor, and all appreciate moist, humid conditions with a medium high in organic content. These plants generally form rosettes of leaves from spreading rhizomes. The flowers are generally inconspicuous, with the leaves being the main show. Plants can easily be propagated by cuttings taken as the rhizome begins to form the new rosettes, much as one would with the very similar-appearing *Tradescantias*.

Where the really phenomenal growth in awareness has come is in the flowering terrestrials such as *Phaius, Spathoglottis, Calanthe, Bletilla*, and others. All have been popular to some extent over the years, but as the demand for potted flowering plants, as well as for exotic garden subjects in frost-free areas, grows, so does the search for new and unusually beautiful orchids of this type. *Phaius tankervilleae*, the nun orchid, may have been the first tropical orchid cultivated in Florida, where it remains among the most popular spring garden subjects.

Large foliage nurseries have taken up the propagation of this species, with stock provided by some of the largest tissue-culture laboratories such as Twyford. Spring now sees a wonderful supply of *Phaius*, well grown in ten inch or larger pots, and sporting a mass of flower spikes. The large, palm-like leaves are lush and luxuriant year-round, and the fat flower spikes emerge in late fall into winter, to give a succession of slightly nodding brown and white blooms offset by rose lips. A green, albino form has recently been more widely propagated. Not only is this plant popular in the frost-free garden, but it is a good subject for the patio in seasonally mild areas where it can be wintered indoors in a sun porch or similar area.

*Spathoglottis* fill a similar niche, though with a smaller plant habit. Again featuring lush palm-like leaves, *Spath. plicata* and a range of hybrids give a spectrum of flower color from soft pink through magenta and onto pure or two-tone yellows. The flowers most resemble small *Cattleyas*, and are borne on upright, gently arching inflorescences that give a succession of bloom over a long period. *Spathoglottis* have been hybridized as garden plants for many years, hence often do not conform to the close naming protocol followed with most orchids. The unfortunate result is many have names that cannot necessarily be traced back to specific parentage. Since

Above: *Masd. gilbertoi*.

most grow under similar conditions, this doesn't really matter, but is frustrating to orchid people who insist on knowing what is behind their plants.

An orchid that is so widely seen that it almost doesn't seem like an orchid any more is *Bletilla striata*, which is often spotted in seed catalogs. Similar in appearance to *Spathoglottis*, but slightly smaller, nearly hidden bulbs will give rise to spikes of lavender or white blooms in early spring, often as the foliage emerges. This is a fairly hardy subject, and has been seen as far north as Philadelphia growing happily from year to year in a garden setting. And of course, the very similarly named *Bletia verrucunda* was one of the first tropical orchids to flower in England.

To compound the indignity of having some of the largest and most diverse genera at the back of the book, in a section devoted to "other orchids," we have one of the most wonderful of all orchids, as well as the genus in which the first man-made hybrid flowered, the *Calanthes*. There are two main types of *Calanthes*: the deciduous, tropical types exemplified by *Cal. vestita*, and the evergreen types so popular in Japan, such as *Cal. masuca*. The evergreen types are not much cultivated in the west, but are highly valued in Japan, where they form a distinct horticultural type. The deciduous types, on the other hand, formed an important part of the cultivated orchid flora of Victorian England, where they fitted right in to the existing conditions.

*Calanthes* were a valued and much-used plant for cut flower as well as for potted plant use in Victorian times. Lack of interest and disease diminished their use for a period of decades around World War II and after, but increased breeding has again made these quite popular with growers. They are easy to grow, doing best under *Cattleya* conditions, with lots of water and fertilizer during growth, tapering off as the often-large bulbs mature. As the leaves, which resemble those of large *Lycastes*, begin to drop, the inflorescence will emerge from the base of the pseudobulb, and rapidly elongate to its upright, arching pose, as flowers open sequentially, usually a few to ten or more at a time. Colors range from white, or white with a red lip, to pink and onto red tones.

As with *Lycastes*, the large leaves indicate a high water use during growth, as well as a need for care so as not to spoil them, though because they are deciduous, damaged leaves will soon not be a problem. The best way to handle *Calanthes* is to pot them each year as new growths emerge. Because backbulbs left attached to the lead bulb—that bulb giving the new growth—will often just shrivel away, pseudobulbs are best divided into singles and crowded into a pot that allows only enough room for each new growth to mature. This "bulb pan" treatment, not unlike what one might do for narcissus or daffodils, will give the maximum "punch" for the space.

## The end

Orchids are the ultimate flowering plants. Only a few of the hundreds of thousands of different types could possibly be paraded before the reader in this space. Some

magnificent plants were not included for a variety of worthy, and not-so-worthy reasons. As with the winner accepting the award, we can only apologize to those whom we did not mention.

Above: *Eriopsis rutidobulbon* is a rare species from Colombia with highly colored blooms on large plants.

# GLOSSARY

**aerial root** – Any root produced above the growing medium.

**anther** – The part of the stamen containing the pollen; the end of the column.

**backbulb** – An old pseudobulb behind the part of a sympodial orchid that is actively growing. Although there may be no leaves the presence of undamaged "eyes" is a sign that growth is possible.

**bifoliate** – Having two leaves.

**cane** – An elongated psuedobulb, usually used when describing *Dendrobiums*.

**crock** – Small pieces of broken earthenware or flower pots, placed in the bottom of a pot when repotting to aid in drainage.

**cultivar** – An individual plant and its vegetative propagations in cultivation; a horticultural variety.

**epiphyte, epiphytic** – A plant which naturally grows upon another plant but does not derive any nourishment from it. Many orchids in cultivation are epiphytic.

**eye** – The bud of a sympodial orchid that will eventually develop into a new lead.

**foliar spray** – Many minor nutrients and trace elements beneficial to growth are best absorbed through the stomata of an orchids leaves when mixed with water and sprayed on the plant.

**genus** (pl. genera) – A natural grouping of closely related species.

**habitat** – The type of place in which a plant normally grows.

**hybrid** – The offspring of a cross between species or hybrids.

**inflorescence** – The flowering portion of a plant.

**intergeneric hybrid** – A hybrid between members of two or more genera.

**keiki** – A Hawaiian word referring to a baby plant produced asexually by an orchid plant, usually used when referring to *Dendrobiums* or vandaceous orchids.

**lead** – An immature vegetative growth on a sympodial orchid that will develop into flower-producing structure.

**lip** – A modified petal of the orchid flower specialized to aid in pollination and different than the other petals.

**lithophyte** – An orchid that grows on rocks.

**medium** – The material in which an orchid is container-grown, it may be organic such as fir bark or inorganic such as lava rock.

**mericlone** – A plant derived from tissue culture that is identical to its parent.

**monopodial** – Orchids which grow upward from a single stem producing leaves and flowers along that stem.

**node** – A joint on a stem or pseudobulb from which a leaf or growth originates.

**panicle** – An inflorescence with a main stem and branches; the flowers on the lower branches open earlier than the upper ones.

**photosynthesis** – The process a plant uses to produce carbohydrates and sugar from water and carbon dioxide in the air using chlorophyl-containing cells exposed to light.

**pseudobulb** – A thickened portion of the stem of many orchids functioning as a water and food storage device.

**raceme** – An unbranched inflorescence of stalked flowers.

**rhizome** – A root-bearing stem of sympodial orchids that progressively sends up leafy shoots.

**scape** – An unbranched inflorescence with one flower.

**sheath** – A modified leaf that encloses an emerging inflorescence or leaf.

**species** – A kind of plant that is distinct from other plants.

**spike** – An unbranched inflorescence of unstalked flowers.

**stolon** – A branch that grows horizontally above the medium and produces roots and shoots at the nodes.

**stomata** – The breathing pores on the surface of a plant's leaves

**sympodial** – Orchids which grow laterally and produce leafy growths along a rhizome.

**terrestrial** – Growing on the ground and supported by soil.

**unifoliate** – Having one leaf.

**velamen** – The thick sponge-like covering of the roots of epiphytic orchids which helps prevent water loss and aids in absorption.

**virus** – A type of infectious agent, much smaller than common microorganisms, several forms of which affect certain kinds of orchids.

## Technical

I do not like having a lot of equipment getting in the way of my subject and myself so the photos in this book were taken with very basic cameras. I use either a Nikon FM with a 55mm f.2.8 Micro Nikkor or a Minolta Dynax 8000i with Minolta's excellent 100mm f.2.8 Macro which focuses 1:1 without any accessories. A few of the double spreads were shot with a Hassleblad 500c with a 100mm f.3.5 Planar.

Professional studio strobes were used for all of the flower portraits. A large 3ft x 4ft lightbank powered by an 800ws DynaLite power pack remains set up in my home studio and is used to photograph our own orchids as they come in to bloom. I usually use one or two additional flash heads for accent or fill-in, with or without softening depending on the subject. For many years I have used an old Thomas 400ws power pack with one flash head with a 16in round diffused reflector for judging and location photography. Sometimes a second flash head would be used for accent. The compact size and fast recycle time of this unit have been especially useful for judging. Recently I have added a DynaLite Uni400 monolight to my equipment. Weighing in at under 4lb, I can fit the flash, tripod, lightstands, 16 x 22 lightbank and all accessories into an easy-to-handle piece of carry-on luggage. Perfect for travel!

All of the photos in this book were shot on transparency (slide) films; Kodachrome, professional and amateur Ektachromes and Fuji films.

## Acknowledgments

This book would not have been possible without high quality subject matter. I would like to acknowledge the following individuals for providing orchids to photograph.

There are many talented orchid growers and fine commercial establishments in South Florida who exhibit at the shows and monthly AOS judging in West Palm Beach at which I do the awards photography. My photo archive would certainly be of poorer quality without the high caliber of orchids that receive awards in this area. I tip my hat to all of the South Florida friends and growers whose awarded orchids I have had the pleasure to photograph.

I would like to thank Gene Monnier of JEM Orchids for allowing me free reign of his greenhouse to photograph paphs and species to round out those chapters.

We do not see many cool-growing orchids here in Florida and I am deeply indebted to my friends Jim and Julie Rassman for arranging a tour of some of the best northwest growers to photograph masdevallias, miltonias, odontoglossums, and unusual cool orchid species. Thanks go out to Theresa Hill of Hillsview Gardens, Marie Riopelle, Dale and Deni Borders, and Patricia Hill of Strawberry Creek Orchids for allowing me to set up shop and photograph any orchids I wanted, and for having such great orchids to photograph. Special thanks to Patricia Harding for providing some unusual species for the camera and acting as photo assistant and gofer during this tour.

Lauris and Jim Rose of Cal-Orchids sent a wonderful selection of *Cymbidiums* and I thank them for selecting such high quality plants. Thanks also to Santa Barbara Orchid Estate for sending some great *Cymbidiums*.

Special thanks to all the girls at Magic Image for providing me fast and dependable photo lab service accompanied by a smile.

None of my recent creative endeavors would have been possible without the support of Kathy. She is always tolerant of my impatience and provides constant encouragement. Her considerable skills as an orchid grower have helped maintain our own orchid collection in prime condition providing many of the fine subjects pictured on these pages.

Finally, had it not been for that small orchid collection my father had on his patio some thirty years ago I might have never been taken by the beauty and diversity of this incredible family of plants. Friends and family generally attribute my artistic talents to my mother. She was always proud of my achievements and would no doubt be extremely pleased with this one. I dedicate this book to the memory of Walter and Audrey Allikas.

## Bibliography

Dressler, Robert L.: *The Orchids, Natural History and Classification*; Harvard University Press,Cambridge, Massachusetts, and London, England, 1981.

Dressler, Robert L.: *Phylogeny and Classification of the Orchid Family*; Dioscorides Press, Portland, Oregon, 1993.

Hawkes, Alex D: *Encyclopedia of Cultivated Orchids*; Faber and Faber, London, 1965.

Withner, Carl L.: *The Orchids A Scientific Survey*; The Ronald Press Company, New York, 1959.

# INDEX